SLOW TRAVEL

Exmoor National Park

Local, characterful guides to Britain's special places

Hila

GW00771904

EDITION 1

Bradt Travel Guides Ltd, UK
The Globe Pequot Press Inc, USA

Bradt

EXMOOR NATIONAL PARK ONLINE

For additional online content, articles, photos and more on the Exmoor National Park, visit
⬚ visit-exmoor.co.uk and ⬚ bradtguides.com/exmoor.

First edition published April 2019
Bradt Travel Guides Ltd
31a High Street, Chesham, Bucks HP5 1BW, England
www.bradtguides.com
Print edition published in the USA by The Globe Pequot Press Inc,
PO Box 480, Guilford, Connecticut 06437-0480

Text copyright © 2019 Hilary Bradt

Maps copyright © 2019 Bradt Travel Guides Ltd; includes map data © OpenStreetMap
contributors
Photographs copyright © 2019 Individual photographers (see below)
Project Managers: Carys Homer & Anna Moores
Cover research: Marta Bescos

ISBN: 978 1 78477 156 0

British Library Cataloguing in Publication Data
A catalogue record for this book is available from the British Library

Photographs
© individual photographers credited beside images & also those from picture libraries
credited as follows: Alamy.com (A); Shutterstock.com (S)

Front cover The South West Coast Path, Great Hangman (James Osmond/A)
Back cover Exmoor ponies (JaklZdenek/S)
Title page Packhorse bridge, Allerford (Christian Mueller/S)

Maps David McCutcheon FBCart.S

Typeset by Ian Spick, Bradt Travel Guides & Pepi Bluck

Production managed by Jellyfish Print Solutions; printed in the UK
Digital conversion by www.dataworks.co.in

AUTHOR

Hilary Bradt co-founded Bradt Travel Guides in 1974, and now lives in semi-retirement in Seaton, east Devon. After 40 years of writing guidebooks to Madagascar and South America, she has embraced her chosen home to the extent of insisting that such a large, varied and beautiful county deserved three Slow guides, not just one. A keen walker, she has hiked many miles of the South West Coast Path and inland footpaths, as well as enjoying Exmoor on someone else's legs – those of a horse. Most Saturdays see her taking part in one of Devon's parkruns (5km, but she's appropriately slow); during the summer, a swim in the sea – just a few minutes away from where she lives – is always a pleasure. Hilary is a productive member of the South West Sculptors Association and lectures regularly on travel-related topics at libraries and literary festivals, both in Devon and further afield.

AUTHOR'S STORY

Exmoor was one of the first place names I knew – it was where Moorland Mousie, hero of one of my favourite pony books, came from, and I desperately wanted an Exmoor pony. A few years later I lived the dream and rode over the huge expanse of those moors, splashing across rivers and cantering along grassy tracks through the bracken. I was hooked. Even the mist and drizzle seemed romantic and my first cream tea extraordinary. It was over 40 years before I returned with a walking group, climbing Dunkery Beacon in a sea of purple heather and picnicking beside Tarr Steps. But only when researching this book did I really start to look at this extraordinary part of the West Country. In a small area it seemed to contain everything I liked best about rural England: dramatic coastal scenery, lovely villages advertising cream teas, little churches full of ancient village art – and Exmoor ponies.

It's a love affair that will last!

CONTRIBUTORS

Janice Booth settled in Devon in 2002 and considers it her 'home county' after many decades living in other parts of the UK. She's fascinated by Devon folklore and history, and has co-written (with Hilary) Bradt's *East Devon & the Jurassic Coast* and *South Devon & Dartmoor*. Her boxes are on pages 60, 62, 74, 88 and 92.

Alistair and Gill Campbell live in Porlock on Exmoor. They walk extensively and have written *Porlock Walks*, a guide to 12 walks in the area. They also volunteer for the National Trust on Holnicote Estate, where their work includes restoring ancient stone walls. Their boxes are on pages 79, 84, 94 and 104.

Victoria Eveleigh (∅ victoriaeveleigh.co.uk) and her husband, Chris breed Exmoor horn sheep and Devon cattle for meat (see box, page 116), as well as Exmoor ponies (see box, page 126). Besides farming, Victoria writes for the *Exmoor* magazine and is an author with Orion Children's Books. Chris illustrates her works. The *Katy's Ponies* series is set on Exmoor, Victoria's standalone novel *A Stallion Called Midnight* is set on Lundy and she has also written *The Horseshoe Trilogy*.

Joanna Griffin likes to combine her passions for wild swimming and writing. She won Bradt's 'My Perfect Day' competition with her description of wild swimming in east Devon, and was a finalist in the 2018 Bradt travel writing competition. She has researched wild swimming throughout Devon and Exmoor. Her contributions are on pages 22, 39 and 59.

A NOTE ON PRICES

Prices for restaurants, cafés and admission change regularly so have not been included, but I have tried to suggest whether a place is an upmarket option or more suited to the budget-conscious. Always check prices beforehand to avoid an unpleasant shock.

ACKNOWLEDGEMENTS

Apart from my beloved contributors who slaved away in their free time for no recompense, and to whom I owe a debt that I can never repay (although I will try), a special thank you goes to Jennette Baxter for information, inspiration and encouragement and Visit Exmoor for their support for this book, the first standalone guide to Exmoor for many years.

I'd also like to thank Jason and Neal of Highcliffe House, Lynton (see ad, page 135), for friendship and local information; Ian and Lorena Mabbutt for local knowledge and for conscientiously eating their way through the best restaurants of southern Exmoor; Penny and Roger Webber at Hindon Farm for using up a bottle of (organic) wine while describing life as organic farmers; and finally the volunteers at museums and tourist information centres (TICs) whose enthusiasm is so infectious.

FOUND SOME NEW SLOW PLACES?

Exmoor is stuffed with people who have specialist knowledge of their part of the West Country and, although I've done my best to check facts, there are bound to be errors as well as the inevitable omissions of really special places. So why not tell us about your experiences? Contact us on ✆ 01753 893444 or ✉ info@bradtguides.com. I will put all updates on to my dedicated webpage (✍ bradtupdates.com/exmoor), as well as adding my own new finds. In addition you can add a review of the book to ✍ bradtguides.com or Amazon.

A NOTE ON MAPS

The numbers on this map correspond to the descriptions in the text, helping you to find your way around. The ♀ symbol indicates that there is a walk in that area. There are also sketch maps for these featured walks.

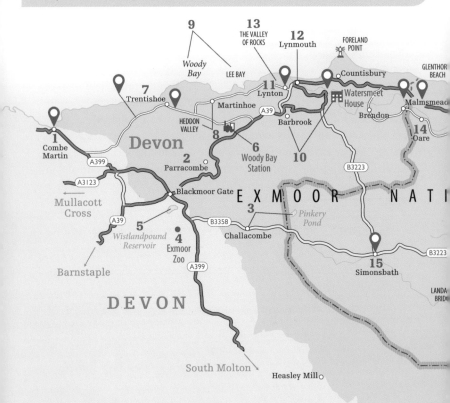

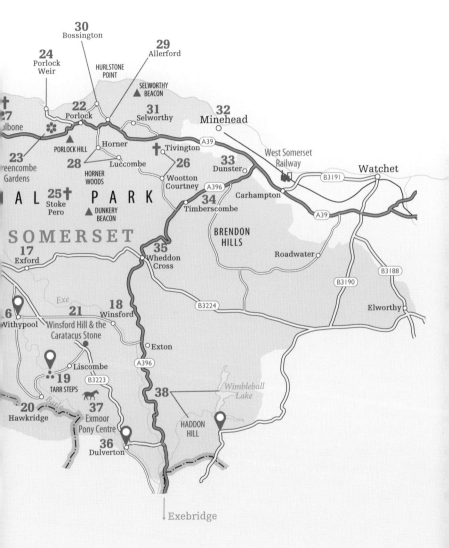

30 Bossington

24 Porlock Weir

HURLSTONE POINT

29 Allerford

SELWORTHY BEACON

27 ‡ ⌐lbone

22 Porlock

31 Selworthy

32 Minehead

23 ⌐eencombe Gardens

PORLOCK HILL

Horner

28 HORNER WOODS

Luccombe

Tivington ‡

26

Wootton Courtney

West Somerset Railway

33 Dunster

Watchet

AL **P A R K** **25** ‡ Stoke Pero

▲ DUNKERY BEACON

34 Timberscombe

Carhampton

B3191

Roadwater

A39

B3188

S O M E R S E T

17 Exford

35 Wheddon Cross

BRENDON HILLS

B3190

Elworthy

Exe

6 Withypool

21

18 Winsford

B3224

19 TARR STEPS

Winsford Hill & the Caratacus Stone

Liscombe

B3223

Exton

A396

Wimbleball Lake

38

20 Hawkridge

Ba⌐le

37 Exmoor Pony Centre

36 Dulverton

HADDON HILL

↓ Exebridge

CONTENTS

EXMOOR NATIONAL PARK

It's impossible not to go slow in Exmoor. From a practical point of view the lack of main-road access and narrow lanes discourage the vroom-vroom mentality, just as the lack of mobile-phone coverage discourages screen addiction. Moreover, the sheer delight of this heathery national park, where moor meets sea, means that visitors can't help but take their time to absorb what they are seeing, talk to locals, indulge in a cream tea and realise that they are in one of the loveliest places in the country. And one which, somehow, has escaped mass tourism.

Of all the experiences I encountered while researching this book, one stands out because it epitomises Exmoor. I had left scant time to do the new (for me) walk described on page 46, which I'd identified on the map as looking ideal in its combination of moor and coast, with one of my favourite churches, Trentishoe, thrown in and the hospitable Hunter's Inn providing a base. It also looked short. It was a late September evening and I disregarded all my own advice, setting out without my hiking pole and boots. Which meant that I *had* to go slowly or risk an accident. No problem – I needed to spend time enjoying the smell of bracken, the sunlight on the heather, and the sight of the Mediterranean-blue sea below sheer indented cliffs. And to stop to look at birds and views through my binoculars. I walked back to my car through an ancient bit of woodland proclaimed by the National Trust to be a 'butterfly trail', though it was now too late to observe insect life. Indeed, it was starting to get dark and I was due to meet friends at a time already past. And, this being Exmoor, there was, of course, no mobile-phone coverage. I asked the barmaid at the busy Hunter's Inn if I could use their landline. No problem, no charge, just friendly helpfulness.

That's Exmoor for you.

THE SLOW MINDSET

We shall not cease from exploration
And the end of all our exploring
Will be to arrive where we started
And know the place for the first time.

T S Eliot, 'Little Gidding', *Four Quartets*

This series evolved, slowly, from a Bradt editorial meeting when we started to explore ideas for guides to our favourite country – Great Britain. We wanted to get away from the usual 'top sights' formula and encourage our authors to bring out the nuances and local differences that make up a sense of place – such things as food, building styles, nature, geology or local people and what makes them tick. Our aim was to create a series that celebrates the present, focusing on sustainable tourism, rather than taking a nostalgic wallow in the past.

So without our realising it at the time, we had defined 'Slow Travel', or at least our concept of it. For the beauty of the Slow movement is that there is no fixed definition; we adapt the philosophy to fit our individual needs and aspirations. Thus Carl Honoré, author of *In Praise of Slow*, writes: 'The Slow Movement is a cultural revolution against the notion that faster is always better. It's not about doing everything at a snail's pace, it's about seeking to do everything at the right speed. Savouring the hours and minutes rather than just counting them. Doing everything as well as possible, instead of as fast as possible. It's about quality over quantity in everything from work to food to parenting.' And travel.

So take time to explore. Don't rush it, get to know an area – and the people who live there – and you'll be as delighted as the authors by what you find.

EXMOOR & THE HAND OF MAN

Exmoor is not a wilderness; from earliest times humans have changed the landscape through their activities. There are a few remnants of Bronze Age barrows, as well as stone circles and standing stones, but nothing like those on Dartmoor where indestructible granite was used.

The climate was warmer and drier in the Bronze Age (2000–650BC), which encouraged people to settle in the sheltered valleys while hunting and pasturing their animals on the high ground during the summer. In Saxon and medieval times small farming communities became established in high valleys, often with a church, showing the influence of Christianity during this period.

The richer, low-lying areas became market towns and centres for the thriving wool industry, and some of the region's great houses were built for rich merchants or members of the aristocracy. Labourers' houses were traditionally built of cob (a mixture of mud, straw and dung) and thatch.

Although farming had been practised since Neolithic times (preceding the Bronze Age), and much native forest cleared for agriculture, the high moors were never suitable for crops. But they were ideal for hunting, and the Royal Forest was established by William the Conqueror. 'Forest', in this case, did not mean woodland but land reserved for hunting and the red deer were protected for the king's pleasure, with draconian punishments for any who killed or harmed them. It was Henry VII who decided to allow the grazing of ponies, sheep and cattle on the moor, provided that at least a hundred deer were left for hunting.

The Civil War and its aftermath diverted attention from hunting (Oliver Cromwell was not known for his pursuit of pleasure) and in 1652 the Royal Forest was sold to James Boevey who built the first house in the Forest, at Simonsbath, enclosing 100 acres of land for his farm. He seems to have spent most of his energies on lawsuits against his neighbours who were using the common land and, even after the restoration of the monarchy in 1660, when all previous crown land once again reverted to the king, he hung on to the farm until his death in 1696.

The greatest change to Exmoor's fortunes came in 1818 when John Knight bought three-quarters of the old Royal Forest and the former Boevey farm at Simonsbath. John and his son Frederic had grand plans for the moor. They aimed to convert some of the heathland to arable pasture and, when this failed, attracted tenants through favourable leases and encouraged them to improve the moorland for the grazing of sheep and ponies. Where arable crops were feasible, they built the beech-hedged walls that are such a distinctive part of the moor today (see box, page 36), and embarked on a programme of road building. They also established mining enterprises, which employed a large number of local people, but these proved unprofitable in the long run and were closed down one by one.

Thus Exmoor's unique beauty was established more from the failure of ambitions than from their success. By the time Exmoor achieved national park status in 1954, large areas of it were already owned by the National Trust.

BAREFOOT & BITLESS RIDING

'Our horses do what we ask them to do,' explained Cathy when we chatted about her innovative approach to horse management. Riding at West Lynch Farm (the Exmoor Owl & Hawk Centre) at Allerford (page 101) is all about the partnership between horse and rider, using a horse's natural willingness to please. Here the horses go 'barefoot and bitless', and some of the saddles used are treeless to give the maximum connection between horse and rider as well as comfort for both. Most horses are ridden in gentle bitless bridles, although sometimes they need the reminder of the control of a bit to reinforce their learning. The barefoot part means the horses are not shod; a special natural diet high in magnesium and low on grass sugars strengthens their feet, bones and joints, and their feet are trimmed regularly to keep them strong. When I commented on the prevalence these days of horse clothing against the weather and flies, Cathy agreed: 'A horse is a horse. We use homeopathy and natural herbs and minerals to help counteract allergies [to insects] and we endeavour to use a full holistic approach with minimal veterinary intervention in their day-to-day care.' The horses also have regular shiatsu sessions.

If you are an experienced rider, have a hack with a difference on Exmoor. It'll be a revelation. ⌀ exmoor-riding.co.uk.

A TASTE OF EXMOOR

Foodies love the abundance of fresh produce and excellent restaurants here, which is partly due to Exmoor's farming heritage and partly due to initiatives such as Eat Exmoor (see box, page 91) which focus on food.

DAIRY TREATS

The taste of Exmoor is undoubtedly that of **clotted cream**. A cream tea is as integral a part of a visit to this region as rain (indeed, the one often leads to the other). Clotted cream is quite unlike any other sort of cream, being as thick as butter and almost as yellow; it contains more fat (around 63%, while double cream is 48%), and traditionally was made by gradually heating fresh milk using steam or hot water, and allowing it to cool very slowly. The thick cream that rises to the top was then skimmed off. The original term was clouted cream, clout being the word for patch, referring to the thick crust that forms when the cream is heated.

Clotted cream is only made in Devon and Cornwall, and we Devonians are not only convinced that ours is better but that we got there first. After all, it was one of the wives of the Dartmoor giant, Blunderbus, who won her husband's affection by bringing the knowledge of clotted-

JULIA AMES GREEN

A TASTE OF EXMOOR

Eat Exmoor is an award-winning initiative that brings together producers, retailers and restaurants in a 'food to fork' initiative.

1 Sheep flourish on Exmoor hill farms. **2** Grown Up Marshmallows is one of several home industries on Exmoor. **3** A Devon cream tea. **4** Wicked Wolf Gin is another flourishing home industry.

VISIT EXMOOR

JULIA AMIES-GREEN

JP@FAYDITPHOTOGRAPHY.COM

cream-making to his kitchen. The story is slightly spoiled by the fact that Jennie was exiled to a cave in Cornwall at the time for being a lousy cook, and it was a Phoenician sea captain who taught her the process as a reward for saving his ship from wreckers.

Clotted cream is served with fresh scones, which should be warm from the oven not the microwave; purists prefer plain scones but others, myself included, love the fruit ones. In Devon we spread the cream on the scone first, instead of butter, and add jam on top; in Cornwall it's the opposite: jam first, then clotted cream. Either way it's utterly delicious – and very filling. The Victorian prime minister William Gladstone was right when he called clotted cream 'the food of the gods'.

Talking of jam, an Exmoor speciality is **whortleberry jam**. Whortleberry is the Exmoor name for bilberry, a heather relative which grows on the moor.

As you would expect by the seaside, there is a proliferation of ice-cream parlours and locally made **ice cream**. One producer in particular stands out: Liscombe Ice Cream (page 73), where you can watch cows being milked by robot while enjoying your cone.

MEAT

Meat eaters are in for a treat here. Some hotels convert to shooting lodges in the winter so pheasant, partridge, woodcock and venison feature on many country menus.

The native cattle could claim to produce the best steak in England. The nickname for the north Devon breed of cattle, **Red Ruby**, is appropriate: these animals are a beautiful chestnut red, the colour of a ripe conker. They are prized for their docility, hardiness and ability to convert grass to succulent, marbled meat. Most of the herds you will see grazing in the Exmoor fields are grown slowly, outdoors (though the climate is such that they need to be brought inside during the winter), with the calves staying with their mothers until they are weaned.

Another native breed, **Exmoor horn sheep**, has adapted to the conditions here over the centuries. And Exmoor has adapted to the sheep, so the landscape you enjoy today owes as much to the grazing of these animals as it does to nature (see box, page 116). The sheep are all-white and, as the name suggests, both rams and ewes have horns. They are dual-purpose animals, raised for wool as well as meat – in the days when mutton was regularly eaten they were considered to have the finest meat of any breed. **Devon closewool sheep** are another breed from Exmoor favoured for meat and hardiness. For more on local meat and where to buy it, see the boxes on pages 50 and 91.

BOOZE

If clotted cream is Devon, then **cider** is Somerset although western Somerset is not in the heart of cider country. For this you need to go east to flatter areas where the cider-apple orchards grow, though small cider producers flourish in our region. Secret Orchard Cider produces award-winning ciders including Exmoor Clear and Exmoor Mellow, as well as the slightly stronger Exmoor Rabbit.

Exmoor also has some small breweries, including Fat Belly in Lynton and Madrigal in Lynmouth, and you'll find these ales in most farm shops and stores selling local products. The largest brewery is Exmoor Ales in Wiveliscombe (⊘ exmoorales.co.uk). Their best-known cask ales are Exmoor Gold and Exmoor Beast but they do a total of ten, some permanent and some seasonal. Also in Wiveliscombe is Cotleigh, whose beers are named after predatory birds: Tawny Owl, Golden Seahawk and Buzzard. They also do seasonal brews such as Rednose Reinbeer.

GROWN UP MARSHMALLOWS

Janet Thomson is the only person I've ever met who makes marshmallows, so my first question had to be why? 'To be honest,' she confesses, 'I'd never been a fan of marshmallows, but then I'd only ever tasted the pink and white variety.' She decided to try making some as a special treat for some students, being confident that she wouldn't eat the lot before they reached their recipients. She was wrong – and marshmallows are now her business, but according to her customers 'too good for children', hence the name.

The mallow plant that is familiar to many of us is indeed an ingredient of marshmallows. 'I use the root in my vegan treats, and fresh strawberries, raspberries, blueberries and blackberries to flavour the fruit marshmallows.' Janet creates her marshmallows at her home in the heart of Exmoor National Park, from natural ingredients that she mostly grows herself. 'I loved the challenge of making a naturally flavoured "perfect mallow" that was firm but soft to the touch, light and fluffy on the tongue, and full of fresh fruit and flavour.' She also uses Fair Trade chocolate and caramel – and even gin.

Grown Up Marshmallows are available to buy from various outlets on and around Exmoor, and can also be purchased online at ⊘ grownupmarshmallows.co.uk.

If it's the stronger stuff you're after, Wicked Wolf Gin is making a name for itself (∂ wickedwolfgin.com). It's run by a husband-and-wife team in Brendon who are proud of the 11 premium botanicals that go into it.

GETTING THERE & AROUND

There is no fast way of getting to Exmoor, only slow. Tiverton is the gateway town, with the A361 speeding car drivers towards the western, Devon section, while east and southern Exmoor is accessed from the A396 which winds its way up the Exe Valley to Wheddon Cross and thence to Dunster and Minehead. The number 398 **bus** follows the same slow route, going from Tiverton to Dulverton, Wheddon Cross, Dunster and Minehead. In addition, the number 198 runs from Dulverton to Minehead via Wheddon Cross and Dunster, and the number 28 goes hourly from Taunton (which is on the main line from Paddington) to Minehead, so eastern Exmoor can be reached relatively easily from London.

The bus's route roughly parallels the **West Somerset Railway** ($\mathscr{D}$ 01643 704996 ∂ west-somersetrailway.co.uk). This is the longest-preserved steam railway in the country, running for 30 miles through some of Somerset's loveliest scenery, from Bishops Lydeard (four miles from Taunton) to Minehead, taking a leisurely 75 minutes. The service runs year-round at weekends and regularly during the summer months, sometimes using diesel engines rather than steam. For an extra treat, step back in time and enjoy a meal on the *Quantock Belle*, a restored first-class dining carriage (page 108).

Apart from the steam train, Exmoor is poorly served by railways, a fact that has contributed to its lack of development. The nearest regular service is the **Tarka Line** from Exeter to Barnstaple, where you can pick up a bus to Lynmouth.

With the demise of the excellent Moor Rover, which used to provide 'on call' transport around Exmoor, there is almost no public transport in the heart of the national park. However, a glimmer of hope lies in the resuscitation of the number 300 bus between Minehead and Lynton. In 2018 this was revived as the **Quantock Heritage Bus**, operating twice a day for a couple of months in the summer. Running along the coastal road, it provides access to some of the most interesting and attractive places in Exmoor, and opens up some 'bus assisted walks'. Concessionary bus passes are *not* accepted on this tourist bus. For information and timetables see ⊘ quantockheritage.com.

ACTIVE EXMOOR

The combination of moorland, forest-lined rivers and rugged coast makes Exmoor National Park the perfect place for some exercise in spectacular surroundings. Visit Exmoor (⊘ visit-exmoor.co.uk) has a section on Active Exmoor that covers cycling, walking, riding and watersports. Exmoor Adventures (⊘ 07976 208279 ⊘ exmooradventures.co.uk; see ad, page 128) in Porlock also runs a variety of courses and days out, from mountain biking to coasteering and kayaking. Similar in scope is Channel Adventure, based in Minehead (⊘ 01643 708715 ⊘ channeladventure.co.uk).

CYCLING

The West Country Way (NCN3) traverses the southern part of Exmoor, going through high moorland, and the many quiet lanes on the moor are ideal for cyclists who don't mind hills (of which there are many) – most of the lanes are wide or across open moor so there's less danger from traffic.

Perhaps the most challenging ride is the 60-mile Exmoor Cycle Route or the linear Culbone Way, Regional Route 51, which runs from Minehead over Exmoor to llfracombe.

Exmoor is ideal for **mountain biking**. Bikes are allowed on bridle paths and RUPPs (Roads Used as Public Paths) but not on public footpaths or open moorland.

Bicycles can be hired in Porlock (page 78) and Minehead at Pompy's (Mart Rd ⊘ 01643 704077 ⊘ pompyscycles.co.uk).

WALKING

Despite its small scale, there are 258 miles of footpaths on Exmoor, including several long-distance paths. This is recognised with the new statue of *The Walker* in Lynmouth. The 102-mile **Two Moors Way** runs from Lynmouth to Ivybridge on the far edge of Dartmoor, or can be extended to the south Devon coast to form a coast-to-coast path; the **Macmillan Way West** (also 102 miles) begins in Castle Cary, enters Exmoor at Withycombe and goes to Barnstaple; the 52-mile **Coleridge**

SHIRLEY TURNER

ACTIVE EXMOOR

Miles of tracks across open moorland, leafy valleys and the open sea make this a perfect region for adventure.

1 Pony trekking. 2 Mountain biking. 3 Walkers on the coast path near the Valley of Rocks.
4 Sea kayaking.

COOL TOURISM

EXMOOR ADVENTURES

OLCO STUDIOS

Way runs from Nether Stowey in the Quantocks to Porlock and then to Lynmouth (download the route description from ⊘ coleridgeway. co.uk). The less well-known **Samaritans Way South West** is a 103-mile route linking Bristol to Lynton. Finally there's the superlative 35-mile Exmoor section of the **South West Coast Path** (SWCP) which begins in Minehead.

Suggested walks are given in each section. If you are planning to do some extensive walking, then it's worth making the most of the best seasons: spring or autumn for woodland or the coast, when the landscape is at its loveliest and the crowds are fewer, but August or early September for the heather. The eastern moor around Dunkery Beacon, and Winsford Hill, Withypool Common and Trentishoe near the coast, are particularly gorgeous, with a mixture of bell heather and ling so that the landscape glows with different shades of purple.

If you prefer a guided walk, these can be organised with the national park (⊘ 01598 751065 ⊘ exmoor-nationalpark.gov.uk); the Exmoor Society (⊘ exmoorsociety.com) also runs regular Exmoor walks, as does Wild About Exmoor (⊘ 01643 831759 ⊘ wildaboutexmoor.com; see ad, page 131) along with other activities. With so many hotels and B&Bs near the main walking routes, few people will choose to carry a tent out of necessity, but there are some wild spots where camping is permitted. You should be aware, however, that no wild camping is allowed anywhere on Exmoor, although there are organised campsites varying from the comfortable to the very rustic.

Walking maps & guides

The Croydecycle walking maps (see box, page 20) at a scale of 1:12,500 cover a good proportion of Exmoor. Details are given in the relevant sections. They include all of the coastal area, while *Coast Path Map 1*, at a scale of 1:15,000, comprises the entire Exmoor stretch of the South West Coast Path from Minehead to Watermouth. If you're driving or cycling, the *Exmoor & Taunton* 1:100,000 map gives you just the right level of detail. The OS double-sided Explorer map OL9 covers all of Exmoor at a scale of 1:25,000 but its size makes it unwieldy to use and the area you want always seems to be on the other side.

A variety of walking guides are available from TICs and Exmoor National Park outlets, but should always be used in conjunction with an OS or (better) a Croydecycle map if available; if you stray off the

CROYDECYCLE MAPS & THEIR CREATOR

Once you've used a Croydecycle map (the name comes from the early maps which were for cyclists, even though walking is now the emphasis) you feel dissatisfied with anything else. There are two 1:15,000 sheets just for the South West Coast Path, but it's the 13 maps that cover the entire North Devon and Exmoor coast at a scale of 1:12,500 or five inches to a mile which are such a joy.

It's not just the scale that makes them special, or the fact that they're small and waterproof, it's their creator Mike Harrison's snippets of explanatory or helpful text. Footpaths might have the warning 'May be muddy after rain' or the reassuring 'sheep grazed' or 'firm grass'. Places of historical or geological interest will have a little block of explanatory text and any other empty space is filled with hard information on buses, phone numbers, and other bits of tourist advice. The maps are regularly updated, and an added bonus is the street plans of some of the larger towns.

Despite his output, with a total of 50 maps on Devon and Exmoor, north Cornwall and west Dorset, this is still a one-man show. When researching a new map Mike will walk up to 20 miles a day, checking out all the footpaths in both directions and taking notes on every feature of use or interest to the walker. The base map comes from six-inch-to-the-mile Ordnance Survey maps published in 1880 and 1905. 'Not that much has changed,' Mike told me, 'but I add information from satellite pictures. Remember, a plan is accurate, a map is about giving the right impression.' An example is that if a map showed roads in their real width in relation to the scale, they would be the thickness of a hair. Junctions may need to be exaggerated for clarity.

CroydeCycle maps are widely available in Exmoor in gift shops and tourist information outlets, but you can also order them direct from ⊘ croydecycle.co.uk.

guidebook's map you'll have difficulty reorientating yourself. *Shortish Walks on Exmoor* by Robert Hesketh and published by Bossiney Books are easy to follow, with clear maps, and are ideal for a brief visit. A useful series of self-published walking guides centred round different popular locations is *Exmoor Scenic Walks* by Shirley and Mike Hesman. The 18 booklets cover all the most popular walking areas of Exmoor; they are cheap, well organised and clearly written, with easy-to-follow maps. Goldeneye Day-Guides – laminated folded card with colour maps – are also useful.

By far the best guide for the South West Coast Path is *Exmoor & North Devon Coast Path* published by Trailblazer. It incorporates the detailed 1:20,000 scale maps which are the publisher's trademark, and includes suggested accommodation.

HORSERIDING

One of my fondest teenage memories is of pony trekking for a week in the 'Lorna Doone country' of Exmoor with my younger sister. I can remember so vividly the woodland rides and the huge sweep of purple moor, and the exhilaration of being able to gallop without worrying about roads or traffic. We started off gently with a couple of hours of morning and afternoon rides, and culminated in a full day trek with lunch at a pub (so grown up!). I can even remember the name of my cob: Satan.

Not much has changed. You can still go for short or long treks across the heather, you can still have lunch in a pub on the long days, and no doubt there are still bolshy cobs called Satan. If you can ride, there's no better way of seeing the moor, and no better way of getting up those steep hills and across the streams.

For the most authentic riding experience, you can take out an Exmoor pony (with some weight restrictions) at the Exmoor Pony Centre in Dulverton (page 120). Another entirely different experience is the 'barefoot and bitless' riding offered at West Lynch Farm (see box, page 12 and page 101).

Finally, if you have your own horse there are several farms that offer accommodation for your horse as well as yourself – indeed, with about 300 miles of bridleway, Exmoor is probably the best place in the country for this sort of holiday. A leaflet available from some TICs lists all the B&Bs that can accommodate your horse, allowing a circular route to be devised (✆ 01643 831151 or ✉ carolecwoods@aol.com for more information).

RIDING & TREKKING STABLES

Brendon Manor Riding Stables Between Lynton & Simonsbath, EX35 6LQ ✆ 01598 741246 ⏇ brendonmanor.com. Also offer horse B&B.

Burrowhayes Farm Riding Stables West Luccombe, Porlock TA24 BHT ✆ 01643 862463 ⏇ burrowhayes.co.uk

Dean Riding Stables Trentishoe EX31 4PJ ✆ 01598 763565 ⏇ deanridingstables.co.uk

Outovercott Riding Stables Nr Barbrook, off the A39, EX35 6JR ✆ 01598 753341 ⏇ outovercott.co.uk

Pine Lodge Higher Chilcott Farm, Dulverton TA22 9QQ ✆ 01398 323559 ⏇ pinelodgeexmoor.co.uk. Also offers riding holidays for unaccompanied children as well as B&B.

West Anstey Farm Stables Nr Tarr Steps, TA22 9RY ✆ 01398 341354

West Lynch Farm Allerford (see box page 12 and page 101)

WILD SWIMMING IN EXMOOR

Joanna Griffin

In recent years, swimming in the wild has increased in popularity. Perhaps it is the sheer sense of freedom, the adventure, and the thrill of exploration that is drawing us to wilder waters. Or maybe it is the uniquely sensory experience of an open-water swim; the pull of a current, the subtle change in light, the brush of weeds or the chill of the water after the rain. Wild swimming enables us to reconnect with the natural world, and with each other, allowing us to travel through our landscape from a different viewpoint.

Whatever it is that is drawing us away from our local swimming baths towards our rivers and lakes, we can be sure that no two swims are ever the same. From deep, shady woodland pools to the more exposed waters of the open moor, wild swimming in north Devon and Exmoor is an experience as varied as the landscape. Whether you're more of a 'dipper' or looking for something longer, wild swimming enables you to experience this lovely region from a different perspective.

Although some swim spots can be accessed more easily than others, the more remote stretches of water are quieter, and locating them is all part of the adventure. There is nothing quite like trekking across open moorland until suddenly an elusive swimming hole comes into view; or finally spotting that hidden stretch of river, long and deep enough for a decent swim. I describe wild swims in the region in boxes on pages 39 and 58, but these are just a sample of what's available.

And of course, there is the sea. This beautiful stretch of dramatic coastline – wild and secluded in parts – offers up deserted bays, family-friendly coves with gently shelving access, and tidal pools, presenting quite a different experience from swimming in fresh water. Here, there are tides to consider as well as wildlife of a different kind, including seals that have been spotted by many a swimmer along the Exmoor coast. Although some stretches of coastline can be busy, particularly the sandy beaches to the west of the region, there are still many opportunities for a truly wild swim. Even if it might involve a scramble down a steep rocky slope with the aid of a rope, or a long trek down rickety steps, swimmers are rewarded by secret beaches and interesting swims through gulleys and caves.

As always when wild swimming, it is important to make sure that the water is safe and that swimming is permitted. A good way of doing this is to use the crowd-sourced wild swim map detailed below, or to join a friendly group of local swimmers with lots of local knowledge and good company.

Further reading & wild swimming resources

Wild Swimming, Daniel Start, Wild Things Publishing, second edition, 2013

⌂ wildswim.com for a crowd-sourced wild swim map.

INACTIVE EXMOOR

Not everyone can – or wants to – jump on a bicycle and pedal furiously up Porlock Hill, and even reasonably fit walkers can find the hills on Exmoor a challenge. They, and the narrow lanes, are a challenge for drivers too, so the alternative is to let someone else take the wheel. The following companies offer safaris in 4x4 vehicles; these give you not only an overview of Exmoor's scenery, but also inside information on its wildlife, traditions and history. Tours last 2½ to three hours, and the route depends on weather and other factors. Because the driver/guides know the moor so well, you have a good chance of seeing red deer.

Discovery Safaris of Porlock ℰ 01643 863444 ⌀ discoverysafaris.com. Trips leave from Porlock in vehicles taking up to six people and last about 2½ hours. Binoculars provided.
Exmoor Wildlife Safaris ℰ 07977 571494 ⌀ exmoorwildlifesafaris.com. Three-hour safaris from Dunster, Dulverton or Exford. Full day by arrangement. See ad, page 128.
Red Stag Safari ℰ 01643 841831 ⌀ redstagsafari.co.uk. Various departure points. Trips last 3½ hours, but all-day safaris can also be arranged, as well as special autumn deer-rut safaris departing from Wheddon Cross. Uses a comfortable Land Rover Discovery vehicle.

WET-WEATHER ACTIVITIES

Combe Martin Museum (page 35)
Dovery Manor Museum Porlock (page 81)
Dunster Castle (page 110)
Guildhall Heritage and Arts Centre Dulverton (page 118)
Exmoor Zoo (page 38)
Liscombe Farm Ice Cream Parlour Tarr Steps (watch milking by robot) (page 73)
Lynmouth Pavilion (page 53)
Lyn Valley Arts & Crafts Centre (page 51)
Lynton & Barnstable Railway (page 40; see ad, page 129)
Rural Life Museum and Victorian Schoolroom Allerford (page 101)
West Somerset Railway (page 16)

FURTHER INFORMATION

Tourist information centres are listed in the relevant towns (Lynton/Lynmouth and Porlock) and Exmoor-specific information is also available from the following:

WEBSITES

Visit Exmoor ⚆ visit-exmoor.co.uk. The first-stop website for all things Exmoor.
Edible Exmoor ⚆ edibleexmoor.co.uk. A really useful website for foodies, showing a wide range of food producers in Exmoor.
Everything Exmoor ⚆ everythingexmoor.org.uk. An information site that is extraordinarily comprehensive, with contributions from members of the public.
Exmoor National Park Authority Dulverton ✆ 01398 323665 ⚆ exmoor-nationalpark.gov.uk
Exmoor Society 34 High St, Dulverton ✆ 01398 232335 ⚆ exmoorsociety.com. Founded 60 years ago, the society organises walks, talks and other events.

BOOKS

Exmoor has a strong literary heritage, with *Lorna Doone* heading the list of books that blend fiction with evocative landscape descriptions. More recently Porlock-based author Margaret Drabble set her novel *The Witch of Exmoor* on her home territory, and one of Exmoor's most venerated characters, Hope Bourne, who died in 2010 at the age of 91, documented her life in the region. She moved to Exmoor on the death of her mother and lived a self-sufficient life spending around £5 a month. Her books, which she illustrated herself, include *Living on Exmoor* and *My Moorland Life*.

Children will love the pony books written by Victoria Eveleigh, farmer, Exmoor pony breeder, and contributor to this guide. Set in Exmoor, they bring the landscape and farming to life, along with the management of Exmoor ponies.

OTHER PUBLICATIONS

Exmoor Magazine ⚆ exmoormagazine.co.uk. In-depth articles of Exmoor interest.
Exmoor Visitor Published by the national park, this tabloid-sized publication repeats in newspaper form the information found on the website. It's free, widely available in shops and tourist information centres, and particularly useful for its detailed list of events.

TWO MOORS FESTIVAL

⚆ twomoorsfestival.co.uk

Every October a most unusual music festival takes place in Exmoor and Dartmoor. Firstly, the music is classical, rather than popular or folk, and secondly it's performed in churches – often quite remote ones that are described in this book. What could be better?

EXMOOR NATIONAL PARK

We came to the great River Exe … which rises in the hills on this
north side of the county … The country it rises in is called Exmoor.
Camden calls it a filthy barren ground, and indeed, so it is; but as
soon as the Exe comes off from the moors and hilly country and
descends into the lower grounds, we found the alteration; for then
we saw Devonshire in its other countenance, cultivated, populous
and fruitful.

Daniel Defoe, 1724

This is still an accurate picture of Exmoor if you change 'filthy barren
ground' for something more complimentary, for it is the heather-
covered moorland as much as the cultivated, populous and fruitful
lower ground that draws visitors. This is one of England's smallest
national parks, a soft landscape of rounded hills, splashed yellow from
gorse and purple in the late summer when the heather blooms, and of
deep, wooded valleys. And Exmoor has the coast, adding pebble coves
and sea views to its attractions, along with the many rivers that race
to the sea from the high ground, slicing into the soft sandstone. With
so much of Exmoor managed by the National Trust, clear signposting
makes walking or cycling a real pleasure. Astonishingly, for such an
utterly delightful region, it's one of England's least visited national parks.
You may not believe this on a sunny weekend in Lynmouth or at The
Hunter's Inn when they're buzzing with
visitors, but solitude is not hard to find.

"Astonishingly, for such a delightful region, it's one of England's least visited national parks."

The publication of *Lorna Doone* in 1869
gave Exmoor tourism a marketing high
that persists to this day, with 2019 seeing
celebrations for its 150th anniversary.
Blackmore's novel is more identifiably set in a genuine English landscape
than most other literary classics, and the number of visitors to Oare
church testifies that fiction is as powerful as fact.

COASTAL EXMOOR

Exmoor: where the moor meets the sea, with hidden coves, sandy beaches and coastal villages.

3

1 The harbour at Porlock Weir has been in use for over a thousand years. 2 The boulders at the Valley of Rocks were deposited during the Ice Age. 3 Combe Martin bay is popular for watersports. 4 The harbour at Lynmouth.

4

Other Exmoor enthusiasts were the Romantic Poets who descended on Exmoor a couple of hundred years ago when Samuel Taylor Coleridge and his pal William Wordsworth tirelessly walked the hills and coast. Coleridge lived in Nether Stowey in the Quantocks, with William and Dorothy lodging nearby. In the autumn of 1797 they walked the coastal path to Lynton, and are said to have planned Coleridge's most famous poem, *The Rime of the Ancient Mariner*, during that walk, with Watchet, east of the national park, being the inspiration for the harbour from where the sailor set out. Coleridge was staying near Culbone when an opium-induced flow of poetry was interrupted by 'a person from Porlock'. He never finished *Kubla Khan*. However, his name lives on in the Coleridge Way, which follows his favourite walk.

In 1799 Robert Southey, the then Poet Laureate, lived in Minehead and penned a rather bad sonnet in praise of Porlock, while nine years later Shelley burst in on the tranquillity of Lynmouth, scattering pamphlets and scandal. All in all, anyone who had anything to do with poetry at the turn of the 18th century seems to have ended up on the Exmoor coast.

THE RED DEER OF EXMOOR

The red deer, *Cervus elaphus*, is the largest native British mammal, with stags nearly four feet high at the shoulder and hinds slightly smaller. Red deer have lived on Exmoor since prehistoric times, and the current population – estimated at around 3,000 animals – is thought to be one of the last truly indigenous populations in the British Isles. For most of the year hinds tend to herd together with their calves in certain areas while stags form bachelor groups, but it's common to find young 'prickets' with hinds and not unusual to find older stags in small groups or even by themselves.

Only the stag has antlers (or horns, as they are called locally), which it sheds in the spring every year. As the animal matures so the annual growth of its antlers increases, adding new points each year until 14 or even 16 points are attained, after which he is usually past his prime and starts to 'go back'. While the antlers are growing they are covered in nutrient-rich 'velvet'. Finding horns that have been shed is a local tradition, and there are often stags' horn competitions at shows during the summer.

All the energy put into growing these antlers is important to achieve supremacy over rival stags during the annual rut from late September until November. The dominant stags round up a harem of hinds, strut around showing off their size, and bellow their challenge to intruders. Fights often ensue. The calves are generally born in June, and to begin with spend much of their time lying concealed

WESTERN EXMOOR: COMBE MARTIN & THE COAST

1 COMBE MARTIN

Combe Martin Museum & Tourist Information Point: Cross St ✆ 01271 889031 ⌂ combemartinmuseum.co.uk ⌚ 10.30–17.00 daily (but dependent on volunteers' availability)

> We passed through Combe Martin, an old, and dirty, and poor place; one house, once a good one, bears the date of 1534; another is built in a most ridiculous castle style and is called The Pack of Cards.
>
> Robert Southey, August 1799

Modern visitors will recognise the Pack o' Cards but not the description of the town as a whole. Squeezed into the crease between two hillsides, within an Area of Outstanding Natural Beauty, this straggly but well-kept town once claimed to have the longest High Street in England. This has now been modified to the longest street party in England, and perhaps the largest number of name changes in one street: five. Once over 70 shops and 19 pubs lined this road; now there are only a handful.

in undergrowth while their mothers graze nearby, returning regularly to let their young suckle. It's very important not to get too close to a calf if you see it, nor touch it, as the hind may abandon it if you do.

You may come upon deer at any time. They are most visible on farmland, where they sometimes congregate in large numbers, but can also be found in woodland and on open moorland (where they are particularly well camouflaged). An organised safari (page 23) will increase your chances as will a guided visit during the rutting season. See *Exmoor Visitor* (page 24) for dates.

There are several places where your chances of seeing deer are good. Alderman's Barrow Allotment (♀ SS836422) is one such place, just off the Exford to Porlock road. Pull off the road and walk south, keeping very quiet and with your eyes peeled. Another area where you may get lucky is along Dicky's Path, which is signed off the road. Park on Stoke Ridge (♀ SS878426) and follow the path southeast. Prayway Head, between Brendon Common and Simonsbath, and the fields and woodlands around Cloutsham are good places to deer watch from a car, and if you feel like a walk large herds can often be found on Soggy Moor near Molland. Sit quietly with the sun behind you and binoculars at the ready, and you will almost certainly be rewarded. For an excellent exhibition on red deer visit the Guildhall Heritage and Arts Centre in Dulverton (page 118).

In the early 19th century Combe Martin was noted by writers, and not just the Poet Laureate Robert Southey, as being run down. Charles Kingsley called it a 'mile-long manstye'. There was a reason, however – landlords deliberately let houses deteriorate to avoid contributing to the Poor Law rates. Inhabitants at that time were called Shammickites, a shammick being a term for a slum.

Nowadays there's plenty to admire here. The town has a long and interesting history. The Martin part of the name comes from Sieur Martin de Turon, who was granted the lands by William the Conqueror. Legend has it that the last Martin failed to come back from a hunting trip so his father, assuming the lad was staying the night elsewhere, ordered that the drawbridge over the moat be raised. The unfortunate hunter returned in the dark, fell into the moat and was drowned, thus ending the Martin line. His father was so consumed with grief and guilt that he left Combe Martin forever.

The family seat passed to the Leys, a descendant of whom built the town's most extraordinary building, the Pack o' Cards.

Once silver ore was discovered in the region, Combe Martin's fortunes blossomed. The first recorded extraction of the metal was in 1292, in the reign of Edward I.

HUNTING THE EARL OF RONE

One of the most bizarre, colourful, historical and highly charged events to take place in the British calendar is Hunting the Earl of Rone in Combe Martin each Spring Bank Holiday (🖉 earl-of-rone.org.uk).

No-one knows how old this event is, but we do know that it was banned in 1837 because of the drunken and licentious behaviour that accompanied it. J L W Page, writing in 1895, describes a conversation with an old lady who remembered the festival with great affection. 'She told me with what an awful joy she would give her halfpenny to escape the jaws of the … hobby horse which laid hold of any non-paying delinquent.'

She is quoted as saying 'My dear soul, I should like to have 'un again!' It was revived, only a little more soberly, in 1973.

The hunt begins on Friday evening, when men dressed as Grenadiers, in scarlet jackets and beribboned conical hats, parade the length of the village, to the beat of drums and the firing of their muskets. Their quarry is a shipwrecked fugitive thought to be hiding out in the woods and subsisting on ship's biscuits. Perhaps he is Hugh O'Neill, the Earl of Tyrone, an Irish traitor who was indeed wanted by the government some 400 years ago. The Grenadiers are accompanied by a Fool carrying a besom, and a Hobby Horse,

Miners had no choice of occupation: they were impressed from the Peak District and Wales to serve various kings and finance their wars in France. Both Edward III and Henry V paid for their claims on French territory through the wealth of Combe Martin. The harbour allowed the metal to be easily transported along with agricultural products, most notably hemp. One of the village industries was the spinning of this hemp into shoe-makers' thread and rope for the shipping industry. More recently, but before refrigeration and polytunnels, the town became renowned for its strawberries, which ripened earlier in this sheltered valley than elsewhere in the country. The mines finally closed for good in 1880. A lively group of volunteers, the CM SM Society, are keeping the history alive through open days and mine visits. Pick up a leaflet at the TIC or contact them (✆ 01271 882442 ✉ cmsmsoc@hotmail.co.uk) for dates.

There are really only two buildings of interest in the town, the **Pack o' Cards** pub and the church, but both are exceptional. The former is a piece of 18th-century eccentricity created by George Ley, a gambler, in homage to his success. All its numbers echo those in a pack of cards, hence its four floors (suits), 13 doors and 13 fireplaces (cards in a suit), and originally 52 windows (cards in a pack); also the

a grotesque twirling figure in a huge, hooped beribboned skirt, a necklace of ship's biscuits and a teeth-clattering horse's head. This procession ends at the 'stable' at the Top George Inn. A miniature (in that it's enacted by children) procession takes place on the Saturday. The highlight of this day is the enormous strawberry cake, celebrating Combe Martin's fruit speciality. Sunday sees another procession, but on Monday things really hot up. After three days of noisy searching, they catch the man in Lady's Wood at the top of the village and, dressed in sackcloth, he is put backwards on a donkey and marched along with drums and music. Now and then he is shot and falls to the ground, only to be revived by the Fool or the Hobby Horse. He's then replaced, again backwards, on the donkey and continues his sad journey, accompanied by maidens carrying flower garlands. Eventually the procession reaches the church where, amid dancing and bells ringing, the Earl of Rone is shot once more. Then it is all the way down to the sea, where the dead Rone (now replaced by a sackcloth effigy), is thrown into the waves from the quay, and the women throw their garlands after him.

The TIC has a good display on this extraordinary festival.

Combe Martin loop: cliffs, beach & silver mines

🌸 Croydecycle *Combe Martin & Hunter's Inn*; start: Combe Martin west-end (beach) car park; 2.6 or 3 miles; moderate (some steep climbs)

This walk is mainly along quiet lanes, though with very few level stretches. It gives you the option of descending to Combe Martin's loveliest cove, Wild Pear Beach, for a swim and also takes you near some reminders of the town's silver-mining past.

Park in the west-end car park near the beach; from the upper end of the car park follow the track signposted South West Coast Path. It climbs steeply uphill to the cliff's edge before turning sharply right, and follows the cliff until you reach the narrow path that leads down to **Wild Pear Beach**, once busy with the traffic of limestone-carrying boats but now blissfully secluded – which is probably why it's popular with naturists.

At the point where the path starts to climb steeply towards **Little Hangman**, look for a turning to the right where you'll join West Challacombe Lane, passing **West Challacombe Manor**, which is now owned by the National Trust and let as self-catering holiday accommodation. This is a beautiful 15th-century manor with a splendid Great Hall, which retains its medieval roof. No-one is certain what it was used for, but it could have housed the miners brought from Wales and the Peak District.

The lane leads to Combe Martin's main street (King Street at this point) so if you want to cut your walk short here you are less than half a mile from your car. To continue, turn sharp left along Hams Lane for a half mile or so, until it curves round and descends steeply to Netherton Cross. You'll catch some lovely views of Combe Martin strung out along its valley. Turn left at the junction then left again, climbing steeply up Knap Down Lane. At the junction with Girt Lane you've reached the highest point and it really is downhill all the way now, as you turn right, then left, then right again to join Corner Lane, which descends steeply into the town. As you start

whole thing looks like a house of cards. Ley, who died in 1709, has a memorial in the **church** of St Peter ad Vincula (St Peter in Chains). Its 100-foot-high tower has been dated at 1490, and was probably built by the same stonemason as neighbouring Berrynarbor and Hartland. A local jingle describes these towers: 'Hartland [in northwest Devon] for length, Berrynarbor for strength, and Combe Martin for beauty.' It is indeed a decorative tower, with statues set in niches. Inside are all sorts of treasures. The rood screen, which dates from the 16th century, has been expertly cleaned to bring out the colours and details of the painted saints in the panels. There are some carved bench ends and

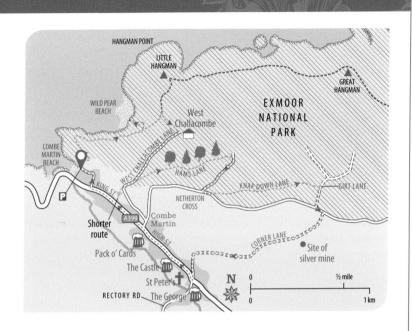

down the lane, look for the tall remains of a **double-cylindered engine house** used in silver mining, a landmark for miles around.

Then it's a just a matter of walking down the High Street/King Street back to your car. However, you emerge close to two pubs, the George and the Castle, so if it's that time of day . . . Or for more spiritual refreshment you're also near the church.

more recent poppyheads (three-dimensional wood carvings) in the choir including a Combe Martin fisherman and a whale. Carved on the capitals above the pillars are the usual vine leaves and grapes, but look out for the rare green woman. On the wall, but too high up to see the detail, is a highly regarded marble sculpture of Judith Ivatt, wearing an exquisitely carved lace collar.

It's useful for visitors to know that there's a general store at the service station near the top end of town (if coming from Blackmoor Gate), a post office not far from the church and its car park, and a small supermarket at the main car park, with the TIC and museum, near

JOHN CHECKLEY

HISTORY & HERITAGE

Ancient remains, literary legends and Devon traditions come together on Exmoor.

1 Cow Castle, an Iron-Age hillfort on the River Barle. **2** The ancient Caratacus Stone on Winsford Hill. **3** Watersmeet House, a former fishing lodge. **4** The statue of Lady Lorna Dugal in Dulverton, the inspiration for Lorna Doone.

@EXMOORNATIONALPARKAUTHORITY

IAN WOOLLOCK/S

CHRISLOFOTOS/S

the beach. This lower end of town is where the beachy shops are, the **Foc's'le Inn** and the **Outdoor Shop** (⬙ outdoorshop-combemartin. co.uk) which hires out paddleboards and kayaks. The lovely little **beach** is composed of sand and shingle, but with enough sand at low tide that you don't need beach shoes for swimming. It's contained within steep tree-hung cliffs making any on-water exploration of the bay particularly rewarding.

Near the beach and car park is the excellent **Museum and Tourist Information Centre**. The museum is full of nuggets of information about the history of the town, its silver-mining industry, and the Hunting the Earl of Rone festival. Children can bring in their finds from the beach to study under a microscope or join an organised beach safari. There are ropes and pulleys to play around with to understand how heavy cargo such as limestone could be loaded on to a boat.

The town has more than its share of **festivals**. A lively carnival is held during the second week of August, when a giant 'grey mare', ridden by Old Uncle Tom Cobley and All, parades around the town on Wednesday evening, presumably looking for Widecombe Fair. There's also a Strawberry Fayre in June, celebrating the town's history as a major fruit-growing region, and the bizarre but hugely enjoyable Hunting the Earl of Rone (see box, page 30), which takes place on the Spring Bank Holiday. 'They like dressing up in Combe Martin,' the lady in the tourist office told me. Indeed!

⏸ FOOD & DRINK

Besshill Farm Shop 4 Borough Rd ✆ 01271 889350 ⊙ 09.00–17.00 Mon–Sat. An excellent selection of free-range meat and fresh vegetables.

Black & White Fish & Chips Borough Rd ✆ 01271 883548 ⊙ noon–14.00 & 17.00–20.00. A long-established, very popular chippie that sells seriously good take-away fish and chips. Located at the beach end of town.

The Pack o' Cards High St ✆ 01271 882300 ⬙ packocards.co.uk. Straightforward food served indoors or in the spacious garden of this unique inn (page 31).

BEYOND COMBE MARTIN

Next to Combe Martin are some of the highest cliffs in the country: **Hangman Cliffs**. Above them are Great Hangman and Little Hangman, and climbing them from sea level is quite a challenge, though the views make it worthwhile. When you stand on the top of Great Hangman, you are at the highest point of the South West Coast Path (1,046 feet). The name comes not from a desperate walker or from the rather appealing alternative, sometimes suggested, that a sheep-thief managed to strangle himself on the animal's rope as he made his getaway. Rather it's a corruption of 'An Maen', Celtic for The Stone or Stony Head. There are some good circular walks that include the peak, but the one described in the box on page 32 cunningly avoids it and gives you some doses of history and a secluded beach, instead of exhaustion.

"The legend is that a sheep-thief strangled himself on the animal's rope as he made his getaway."

If you decided to do the hard slog to the top of Great Hangman you may be tempted to continue east along the South West Coast Path. This is, after all, perhaps *the* most spectacular and varied stretch of the entire route. However, there is no bus link until you reach Lynmouth, 13 miles away; given the hilly terrain, this is a lot to do in one day. A good solution is to split the walk into two days, staying overnight at the welcoming Hunter's Inn (page 45).

HEDGES, TREES & WALLS

There is a saying that for every species of tree in a hedge you can add another hundred years to its age. Hedges served a dual purpose: they contained cattle and sheep in pasture, and they provided edible berries for rural households. Thus hawthorn, blackthorn (for sloes) and blackberry were popular, their spines making an effective barrier. Beech was introduced in the 18th century, having the advantage of keeping its dead leaves in the winter, so maintaining the visual effect of an impenetrable barrier. Earth banks were also constructed to provide shelter for flocks in Devon's stormy weather and faced with stone for stability. They were planted with beech trees to give additional height. Traditionally these were pollarded or cut and laid but, once mechanical flayers made this labour-intensive task uneconomical, the trees grew unchecked and are now a common sight in Devon, their roots straddling the bank. Sycamore was introduced in the 1600s, as a fast-growing, salt-tolerant species but, compared with the native oak, it is a poor host. Where an oak can support up to 200 species of insect, the sycamore is home to only 12.

Dry-stone walls are also a feature of the North Devon countryside, and the skill with which they were built is testified in their age: 200 years or more. The Dry Stone Walling Association of Great Britain is involved in encouraging the continuation of this traditional craft and you will see some beautiful examples of new walls as well as ancient ones.

THE INLAND ROUTE: TO LYNTON VIA BLACKMOOR GATE

When you're approaching Exmoor from the west, all roads seem to lead to Blackmoor Gate, and from there most drivers heading east towards Lynton take the relatively uninteresting A39. From this route, however, the church at Parracombe really shouldn't be missed by anyone who loves old churches. Those approaching (or leaving) Blackmoor Gate via the A399 have two worthwhile diversions: **Challacombe** for its famous pub and walks (including to a longstone and some wild swimming); and **Exmoor Zoo**.

Blackmoor Gate itself has its place in history. It was once an important railway station on the narrow-gauge Barnstaple-to-Lynton railway, and a livestock market (mainly sheep) is still regularly held there (⊘ exmoorfarmers.co.uk). The preserved two-mile stretch of this railway, down which shiny little steam locomotives currently puff their way from Woody Bay Station to Killington Halt (page 40), is scheduled to be extended, which will (if it takes place) bring trains and their passengers to Blackmoor Gate once again.

2 PARRACOMBE

Cupped within a bulge of the A39, and almost lost in a maze of steep, narrow lanes, is this lovely little village with two churches and an excellent pub (page 40). The old church, **St Petrock's**, is rightly the one that draws visitors. It was scheduled for demolition in 1878 when a more conveniently located church had been built, but was saved after a protest led by John Ruskin and is now cared for by the Churches' Conservation Trust.

"They're more like slightly wobbly cairns than stone-mason's art, and all the more charming for it."

It stands high above the village, overlooking its usurper church and the scatter of white houses, with the fields of north Devon stretching to the horizon. The squat tower is a landmark from the main road, the pinnacles looking as though they were added as an afterthought by a farmer. They're more like slightly wobbly cairns than stone-mason's art, and all the more charming for it. Inside, the church is plain and unadorned. No-one has 'improved' it, but it is clearly cared for and cared about. The first thing you notice on entering is the wooden 'tympanum', boldly painted with a royal coat of arms and improving texts: the Ten Commandments and the Creed. The only carving is the screen and even this is less intricate than usually found in Devon churches. The plain box pews are rough with old woodworm, and at the back there's a musicians' area where a hole has been cut in the pew in front to allow free movement for the bow of the double bass. Note, too, the hat pegs by the door.

3 CHALLACOMBE & PINKERY POND

Apart from the famous Black Venus Inn (page 40) and its well-stocked village store, **Challacombe** is best known for the nearby **longstone**, the most spectacular prehistoric monument on Exmoor, standing nine feet high and remarkably slender. It's marked on the OS Explorer map OL9 (♀ SS70514307) and you'll need this map, or the Challacombe booklet in the *Exmoor Scenic Walks* series, to find it. It's a mile or two from the road (the B3358), northeast of Challacombe, near the source of the River Bray. It used to stand in a hollow that filled with water after rain, and a nearby spring made it even wetter; archaeologists levelled it off with gravel in 2003, but the area around it is still very marshy, so be prepared with the right footwear if you decide to look for it.

"Challacombe is best known for the nearby longstone, the most spectacular prehistoric monument on Exmoor, standing nine feet high."

To the east of the longstone, and only a mile from the road, is **Pinkery Pond**, a lovely place for a wild swim (see box, opposite) and the source of the River Barle. Pinkery used to be Pinkworthy (though always pronounced Pinkery), but that spelling is now lost. Nearby is the **Pinkery Centre for Outdoor Learning**, run by the national park, which introduces youngsters to every aspect of Exmoor's wild side.

4 EXMOOR ZOO

South Stowford, Bratton Fleming EX31 4SG ✐ 01598 763352 ⚭ exmoorzoo.co.uk
⊙ 10.00–18.00 (summer) or until dusk (winter) daily, except 3 days at Christmas

Off the A399 is this well-managed zoo. A black leopard, thought to be the Exmoor Beast of local legend, is the most promoted exhibit (though melanistic big cats such as this are not that unusual), but there are 175 species in total, some of which are rarely seen in zoos, with intriguing names such as Chacoan mara, New Guinea singing dog,

WILD SWIMMING IN PINKERY POND

Joanna Griffin

Pinkery Pond, situated on the bleak northwestern plateau of Exmoor known as The Chains, really is a remote spot for a dip. Formed in 1830 by the damming of the River Barle near its source and occupying around 3 acres, it is large and deep enough (reportedly 30-foot-deep in parts) for a long swim. In the southeast corner is a tiny gravelly beach that gently shelves down into the water, providing easy access to the red, peaty depths. Just beside this entry is a narrow moss- and fern-clad tunnel cut into the rock, through which the shallow stream flows into the river.

It is a bit of a trek across boggy moorland to reach the pond, but well worth the effort. It's clearly marked on the OS map at ♀ SS72364230.

From Goat Hill Bridge on the road between Challacombe and Simonsbath, pass through the gate and follow the road to the right of the River Barle towards the Pinkery Exploration Centre. Take a track to the left just before the centre, and pass through a copse of trees on the other side of the field, before reaching open moorland. From here, continue along the stone track that winds alongside the infant Barle, watching the river becoming increasingly narrow as you climb. The pond will suddenly come into view as you reach the bridleway between Wood Barrow Gate to the west and Exe Head to the east.

You could combine your swim with a visit to the prehistoric longstone, which can be reached by returning to Wood Barrow Gate and heading due west.

and dusky padamelon. Animal welfare and breeding of endangered species have high priority, so animals are given the chance to hide within their enclosures. To counteract any visitor disappointment at not seeing their favourite, there are animal encounters with easy-going creatures such as tapirs and wallabies, and the opportunity to be a keeper for a day.

This is an exceptionally child-friendly zoo, even to the extent of having a lost-child trail so small children can find their way back to the entrance. A great idea!

5 WISTLANDPOUND RESERVOIR

North of the zoo is this pleasant lake surrounded by conifers and encircled by trails. It's popular with dog-walkers and runners, and accessible to buggies and wheelchairs since the paths are tarmacked. The car park furthest from the reservoir is free; there is a charge for the one by the lake.

¶¶ FOOD & DRINK

The Black Venus Inn Challacombe EX31 4TT ✆ 01598 763251 ⟨⟩ blackvenusinn.co.uk.
This lovely 16th-century pub is a good reason to visit Challacombe. Hearty meals of nicely
presented, traditional pub food, with a few unexpected treats and a great atmosphere.
Dog friendly.

Fox and Goose Parracombe EX31 4PE ✆ 01598 763239 ⟨⟩ foxandgooseinnexmoor.co.uk.
Recommended for its exceptional food and wide range of beers. The décor is genuine Exmoor,
with foxes' masks and deer antlers, as well as antiques; the food is locally sourced where
possible and traditional as well as imaginative. As popular with locals for conversation as for
food. Dog friendly.

6 WOODY BAY STATION

EX31 4RA ✆ 01598 763487 ⟨⟩ lynton-rail.co.uk

Although currently only two miles long, this narrow-gauge railway
is the highest in England and its trains puff their way through some
of Exmoor's best scenery, making it a rewarding family excursion or
a nostalgic trip for oldies. The enthusiasm of the volunteers who
run this stretch of the original Lynton & Barnstaple Railway, which
operated from 1898 to 1935, is evident in every detail, from the loving
maintenance of the steam locomotives to the tea room. The station was
originally planned to serve the actual Woody Bay (or Woodabay, as it
was then called), nearly two miles away, with a branch line, as part of the
scheme to make Woody Bay a major tourist attraction (page 47).

In 2018 the park authorities gave permission to extend the line west to
Blackmoor Gate and eventually on to Barnstaple, recreating its original
route, but there is fierce opposition from some landowners so whether
this will actually be achieved is uncertain.

THE COASTAL TRIANGLE

Between Combe Martin and Lynton the A399 and A39 roads form the
southern edges of a triangular slice of Exmoor of quite extraordinary
beauty. No serious road builder was going to give priority to this chaos
of moorland, hills and valleys when a more level highway to the south
had served its purpose for centuries. As you approach the deep Heddon
Valley, with its popular The Hunter's Inn, driving becomes increasingly
challenging, as does walking: the hills are *very* steep. But the scenery,
in all its Exmoor variety, is sublime: high moor, ancient meadows and

LYME DISEASE

Lyme disease is carried by ticks, and is a risk when you're walking in particularly brackeny country where there are also livestock such as deer. The most common early symptom of Lyme disease is a rash of red spots, which gradually spreads from the site of the tick bite. It may appear as much as four weeks after the tick has been removed. Occasionally a flu-like illness develops but more commonly there are no further symptoms until some months after the bite, when neurological symptoms may start to develop, including facial palsy, viral-type meningitis and nerve inflammation. Encephalitis (swelling of the brain) is a rare complication.

Remember that most tick bites are harmless, and if you don't develop the rash you have little cause to worry. However, it's sensible to protect yourself with insect repellent. Long trousers are usually recommended but ticks can often find their way to your skin undetected. You may be better off wearing shorts and checking yourself at regular intervals. It takes ticks a while to get established. Carry tweezers with you, and if you do find a tick remove it carefully, ensuring that its mouth parts are not left in the skin to cause infection. If you develop the tell-tale rash, see a doctor as soon as possible.

hanging woods of sessile oaks, accessible by lanes so steep and narrow that even devoted drivers will feel challenged. The coast, tracked by one of the most scenic stretches of the South West Coast Path, is indented with shingle beaches hidden by high cliffs. Altogether an area not to be missed.

7 TRENTISHOE

Trentishoe is one of those isolated communities that make Exmoor so special. It is best accessed from the west to avoid a near-vertical hill from Heddon Valley (now marked 'unfit for motors'). The drive there along the narrow lane from Combe Martin is in the lead for the most dramatically beautiful in Exmoor – particularly if the heather is in bloom, when bursts of purple plus yellow from the gorse alternate with sea views.

Shortly before the scatter of houses and a church that make up this hamlet you pass between Holdstone Down and Trentishoe Down, both of which have some good walking possibilities (see box, page 44).

Chiselled into the hillside is **St Peter's Church**: tiny and, at first glance, pretty ordinary. But at first sniff it's not ordinary: it smells. Bats have taken over the interior, and as protected species it is compulsory for churches to make them welcome. The human congregation who attend

NIGEL STONE

WOODLAND

Although Exmoor conjures up images of heather-covered moors, deep valleys and woodlands are also part of its appeal.

1 Gnarled trees and bluebells make a fine display in May. **2** Tarr Steps, Exmoor's famous clapper bridge. **3** Exmoor's popular walks are well signposted. **4** Pied flycatcher. **5** Part of the annual display in Snowdrop Valley. **6** The East Lyn River.

PETER TURNER PHOTOGRAPHY'S

SANDRA STANDBRIDGE'S

PETE RAE

VISIT EXMOOR

Trentishoe Down: coast, woods & moor

✺ Croydecycle *Combe Martin & Hunter's Inn*; start: The Glass Box car park, Trentishoe Down
⚲ SS62614767, postcode EX34 0PF or, for the shorter walk, the next car park to the east
⚲ SS6348748017; 2½ miles or 2 miles; moderate to strenuous

This delightful walk encompasses a short section of the South West Coast Path (SWCP), a lovely level stroll through woodland, and a climb up to heather and gorse moorland. Don't be fooled by the apparent short distance, however. It took me nearly two hours because of the steep descent and ascent. The walk can be shortened by omitting the coast path section.

The house aptly named '**The Glass Box**' makes a convenient landmark for finding the car park on the north side of Trentishoe Down. Before starting your walk, if the weather is clear, you might want to climb up to **Trentishoe Barrow**, a Bronze-Age burial mound, though there is nothing to see here these days except a fine view. A faint path leads up beside the fence of the Glass Box, bearing left after a few yards (so don't follow the clearer path along the fence), and continuing up to the cairn, which marks both the barrow and the highest point on Trentishoe Down.

The walk proper starts from the car park, where a path runs north to meet the SWCP – here you turn right towards **The Hunter's Inn** (signposted) and follow the stony trail, with lovely sea and cliff views, before taking the path signed County Road to the next car park (where you will park if doing the shorter walk). At the Holdstone Down signpost turn right, following the National Trust sign along the road until you come to the footpath to **Trentishoe Manor** on the right. Follow this steeply downhill, first through bracken and then past some magnificent old beech trees that were once part of a wall (see box, page 36). The level stretch of Ladies Mile comes as a relief as it contours the side of the hill, passing through lovely groves of silver birch and oak.

the occasional service co-exist with them as best they can. Visitors, however, love the bats and the negative comments I used to see in the visitors' book have been replaced by warmly positive ones. This tiny village has supported its church since 1260 (though most of the present-day church is a Victorian restoration) and bats are expensive guests so perhaps you can spare a bit more than usual for the upkeep box.

Apart from the bats the church has a unique feature. In its musicians' gallery is a hole cut in the woodwork to allow for the bow of the double bass. There's a similar one at Parracombe, but I believe this is the only one in a gallery – so many such galleries were removed by Victorian 'restorers'. The little organ came from the ocean liner the RMS *Mauretania*, which was scrapped in 1965.

The path was cut into the side of the hill in Victorian times, supposedly so the ladies of Trentishoe Manor could walk to church.

Just before reaching the road and manor, look out for an unsigned path forking right through the trees. Follow this steeply uphill, a hard slog of 20 minutes or so, first through woodland, then bracken, and finally heather and gorse. Don't forget to look back at the super view. You'll reach a broad farm track that links Tattiscombe

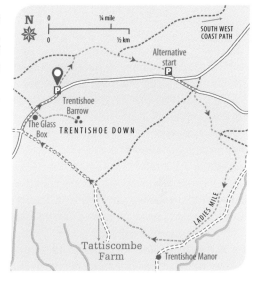

Farm with the coastal road. If you left your car at the first car park you need to follow this track to the road where you turn right, past the Glass Box. If doing the shorter walk, however, take the fainter track to the right. This climbs up over Trentishoe Down and comes out on the road by the path down to the Ladies Mile, a short distance from the second car park.

8 THE HUNTER'S INN, HEDDON VALLEY & MARTINHOE

The Hunter's Inn, in the deep fold of **Heddon Valley**, was originally a thatched cottage that served ale to thirsty workers in this isolated place, but when it burned down in 1896 Colonel Lake (page 48) funded a new design based on a Swiss chalet. It has now morphed into something more in keeping with the scenery and is deservedly the most popular and best-known inn on Exmoor. Its future was secured in 2018 when it was bought by the National Trust, who now manage the whole valley. The food has always been good here, and promises to be even better when the Trust achieve their plans to use produce from their farm at Kipscombe.

The Hunter's Inn & Trentishoe Circuit

✳ Croydecycle *Combe Martin & Hunter's Inn*; start: The Hunter's Inn; 3½ miles; strenuous

This tough walk brings you through some of the most sublime and varied scenery in Exmoor. Perhaps *the* most sublime, so you won't mind your bursting lungs as you climb the hills or your knees aching as you slither down them. It takes you through wooded valleys and along a superb stretch of coast path, purple with heather in the summer, close to the cliff edge (so if you're afraid of heights, this might not be for you). There's also the opportunity to visit little Trentishoe Church and its resident bats.

The description below has the long descent on a rough and stony path, though often with steps; many people find it easier to go uphill on rough terrain, in which case just reverse the route; it's very easy to follow.

Park at **The Hunter's Inn** car park. Walk past the inn on your right along Joses Lane, crossing first the River Heddon and then Trentishoe Water. Take the right turning up the lane towards Trentishoe Church. As you gasp your way upwards you'll realise why it's recently been declared unfit for motors: it's very steep. The path to the South West Coast Path is on your right, towards the top of the hill before the few houses and farms that comprise Trentishoe, but the church deserves your visit and is only five minutes or so further on.

Retrace your steps to the footpath, which is grassy underfoot, through bracken, with grand views of the wooded **Heddon Valley** to the right. It's close on a mile of easy walking before you meet the coast path where you turn right, following a stony trail along the cliff edge where the view of sea, headland and heather (in the summer) is absolutely gorgeous. Being the SWCP

A spacious picnic area surrounded by woodland completes the scene.

The Hunter's Inn is the start or finish of several outstanding walks, all taking in sections of the South West Coast Path, and all involving strenuous hill climbing. The mile-long walk to Heddon's Mouth, down the gorge-like Heddon's Cleave, is the exception, being blissfully level and ending with the opportunity for a swim. Leading off from The Hunter's Inn is the Old Carriage Way, a broad track taking you up and along the cliffs for some of the best views on Exmoor. The path passes The Beacon, which was a Roman fortlet or lookout post.

On the opposite side of Heddon Valley, up another alarming hill, is **Martinhoe**. This hamlet consists of a few houses, the Old Rectory Hotel (see ad, page 134), and a peaceful church. There is little else to it apart from height and scenery, and it's none the worse for that.

it's carefully made, mostly following contours and with steps down the steepest part, but you still need to take care on the pebbles. The last part of the descent to the valley, still following the SWCP, is along the NT's '**butterfly trail**' through woodland, before meeting the Heddon Valley trail where you turn right to follow the river to Joses Lane and The Hunter's Inn for some well-deserved refreshment.

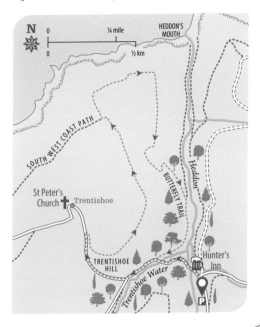

To reverse the route, take Joses Lane towards Trentishoe Hill, turning right just after the second river crossing. The SWCP, up the butterfly trail, is signposted to the left, first through woodland, then steeply up to the cliff top.

9 WOODY BAY & LEE BAY

Beyond Martinhoe the road continues east towards **Woody Bay**, a secluded horseshoe-shaped cove overhung with woods, through which a waterfall plunges. Its name has become inappropriately prominent in Exmoor through the efforts of a 19th-century solicitor, Colonel Benjamin Lake, who had plans to make it a major tourist attraction to rival Lynmouth. In 1895, J L W Page explained that the new road to what is now Hunter's Inn 'is the work of a syndicate, who are, it is said, going to do great things at Woodabay – towards the opening up (and probably cockneyfying) of this shady retreat. When I was last there an engineer was already busy taking soundings for a landing stage. As there are only six houses … the enterprise seems, as the Americans would say, a little previous.' Indeed it was, but it was storms that put paid to the plan, not the small population. A pier was indeed built in 1895. Lake's plans were for a 100-yard-long pier with a dog-leg extension and landing stage, but eventually he could only afford 80 yards. It was completed for the arrival of the first pleasure steamer in 1897, but the steamers were unable to dock at low tide and the service was sporadic. Three years later, storms had all but destroyed the pier and it was finally pulled down in 1902. Colonel Lake also funded a replacement for the original Hunter's Inn (page 45). He ended in bankruptcy and, having used some of his clients' money for his project, prison.

"The 800-foot descent from the little car park on the road above is enough to deter most people."

These days, Woody Bay has its attractions but is really only worth visiting at mid-to-low tide when there is some sand. The 800-foot descent from the little car park on the road above is enough to deter most people, though SWCP walkers will find it worth the relatively short diversion. A swim here is the reward for your efforts, with the surrounding rocks and overhanging woodland making an appealing view from the sea. Beware of trying to rinse off under the waterfall: the rocks are *very* slippery.

The lazy option is to drive or walk west to **Lee Bay**. This private shingle cove is the most accessible in the region, with parking nearby and the lovely **Tea Cottage** providing snacks and cream teas. A toll road beyond the bay takes you to the Valley of Rocks (page 57) and on to Lynton and Lynmouth.

LYNTON, LYNMOUTH & AREA

Without doubt this is the most popular part of Exmoor – and deservedly so. It really does have everything, and all within walking distance: a pretty seaside village, a cliff railway, a tumbling river cutting through forested slopes, the heather-clad moor, and a dollop of recent history. Painters and poets have rhapsodised about its beauty: Gainsborough thought it the perfect place to paint, and Shelley (see box, page 56) lived in Lynmouth for nine weeks with his first wife. Writing in 1928, S P B Mais felt that: 'Ordinary standards simply won't do to describe this corner of Devon. One realises dimly and dumbly that no other combe of one's acquaintance comes quite so obligingly near to the hotel door to show its beauty of wood or majesty of cliff.'

Lynmouth was 'discovered' in the early part of the 19th century when the Napoleonic Wars had closed the continent to English visitors, and the English gentry had to be satisfied with holidaying nearer to home. The Rising Sun Inn was already there to cope with this influx and other inns were hastily built, but it seems that once the war was over, there was fierce competition between the three lodging houses for potential customers. Murray's travel guide of 1856 warns that: 'telescopes are employed at the rival houses for the prompt discovery of the approaching traveller. He had better determine beforehand on his inn, or he may become a bone of contention to a triad of postboys, who wait with additional horses at the bottom of the hill to drag the carriage to its destination.' When you look at the hills they had to climb you can see why additional horses were required. Stagecoaches continued to be used here well into the 1900s; the hills were too steep and too rough for the new-fangled charabancs.

"When you look at the hills they had to climb you can see why additional horses were required."

The popularity of the village was noted, somewhat sourly, by J L W Page in 1895. 'Lynmouth consists of a single street facing the river. Every other house is a hotel or a lodging house [not much change there, then], but the general appearance of the place is not unpicturesque, and some regard has evidently been had for the romantic surroundings.' He points out that Lynmouth was once the centre of herring fishing until, in 1797, 'they suddenly departed. So Lynmouth had to fish for other fry, and does it pretty successfully. Every year does the shoal of visitors increase, and probably they pay better than herrings.'

The publisher Sir George Newnes lived in Lynton, at Hollerday House, and gave the town its cliff railway in 1890, as well as its town hall. Newnes founded the racy magazine *Tit-Bits* and followed it up with the altogether more serious *Strand Magazine*, which was the first to publish Sherlock Holmes stories.

In addition to its other attractions, this area is superb for walking, comprising not only cliffs and moorland but a selection of walks, both circular and linear, along the beautiful East Lyn River and its accompanying woodland. Indeed, Croydecycle's Mike Harrison believes 'There's no better place to walk in Britain than this area.' Just two sample walks are described here; buy Mike's *Lynton, Lynmouth & Doone Valley* map and devise your own.

10 BARBROOK & WATERSMEET HOUSE

Lynmouth is almost encircled by the A39 and accessed down dramatically steep hills, bearing the brunt of through traffic to Porlock, while Lynton, to the west of the main road, is quieter. All traffic passes through **Barbrook** with its handy service station, and farms nearby that are rearing some of Exmoor's very best meat (see box, below).

The less precipitous road to Lynmouth and beyond is Watersmeet Road, which takes you past one of the area's most popular tea rooms, the National Trust-operated **Watersmeet House** (☉ Easter–Oct daily, Nov–Easter Sat & Sun). Most people walk here from Lynmouth (see box, page 58) but there is a (paying) parking area on the road above

MARVELLOUS MEAT

Two farmers near **Barbrook** raise animals that lead as natural lives as possible, providing the highest quality meat that can be bought direct from the farms. Other meat producers are listed in the box on page 91.

Hidden Valley Pigs (Hidden Valley Farm, Barbrook EX35 6PH ✆ 07870 724042 ◌ hiddenvalleypigs.co.uk) is the enterprise of Simon and Debbie Dawson, who swapped their London lives as estate agent and solicitor for rural Devon. Their smallholding focuses on rare-breed Berkshire pigs, and the Dawsons offer a variety of courses including a pig butchery and processing weekend. They also offer 'Rear a Pig'. Sadly this doesn't mean you take your piglet home with you – it remains at the farm, growing slowly and naturally, foraging in the woodland, and more or less writing progress reports to its mum. (Debbie ensures that you are kept properly informed of its wellbeing; you even have visiting and naming rights if you want.) When the time comes, the slaughterhouse is only a few miles away and the pigs get a special treat the night before.

Simon is the author of several books, including *The Sty's the Limit* and *Pigs in Clover*. The couple are currently building an off-grid ecohouse on their land – which will no doubt provide plenty of material for another book.

Victoria and Chris Eveleigh live about a mile away from Simon and Debbie, farming 'red ruby' Devon cattle and Exmoor horn sheep at **West Ilkerton Farm** (✆ 01598 752310 ◌ westilkerton.co.uk). Their animals are born and raised on the farm, grass-fed, allowed to mature slowly and given a life that is as happy, healthy and natural as possible. The Eveleighs use the local abattoir at Combe Martin and transport their animals there themselves to ensure minimal stress at all times. The result is wonderfully succulent meat that can be ordered fresh in advance or bought frozen at any time, subject to availability. The Eveleighs sell their meat in a variety of selection boxes, and sometimes also have individual cuts available. Their gluten-free beef sausages and burgers are especially popular. During the summer months tours are available around the farm.

with a steep path down. Everything about this former fishing lodge is perfect: the choice of snacks and cakes, and especially the location.

11 LYNTON

Tourist information: Town hall, Lee Rd ✆ 01598 752225 ⟁ visitlyntonandlynmouth.com
⊙ days/hours vary seasonally

Lynton's sturdy Victorian houses and extraordinary town hall are surprising in a place that otherwise feels like a modern, upmarket holiday centre. The **town hall** is described in *The Shell Guide* of 1975 as 'a jolly edifice, "15th century" stonework, "Tudor" half timbering, and "Flemish" barge boarding'. Today, as well as the town council, it houses the Tourist Information Centre. The former Methodist Church has been put to good use: the church itself houses the rewarding Lyn Valley Arts and Crafts Centre and the hall is now a cosy 70-seat **cinema**, a charming place run by volunteers.

Lynton has a particularly good selection of accommodation, most with superb views, and some excellent shops and restaurants (page 52). Even with such a range of craft shops the **Arts and Crafts Centre** (⊙ 10.00–17.00), next to the town hall, stands out for its range of high-quality but affordable crafts, which includes preserves, honey and soap.

"The cliff railway is a masterpiece of simple engineering and a model of 'green' energy."

Notable shops include **Lyn Candles** on Lee Road, selling a huge range of the eponymous things with great enthusiasm, the **Lynton Sheepskin Shop**, also on Lee Road, with a comprehensive range, and **John Arbon textiles** down Queen Street with lots and lots of pure wool socks.

Linking Lynton and Lynmouth is the **cliff railway**, a masterpiece of simple engineering and a model of 'green' energy. The two carriages are counter-balanced by water. Fill the tank at the top, and it's heavy enough to pull the other carriage up as it descends. We watched the 'driver' at the bottom judge the amount of water to let out to counterbalance not only the weight of the carriage but the passengers as well. Really neat, and a great way to get to the top of a 500-foot cliff. The year 2015 marked 150 years of continuous operation. Dogs and bicycles are allowed. Before the road was built in 1828, tourists were transported to Lynton on donkeys or Exmoor ponies, as were all the goods arriving in the harbour.

🍴 FOOD & DRINK

The Cottage Inn Lynbridge EX35 6NR ☎ 01598 753496 ⊘ thecottageinnlynton.co.uk. This is a restaurant with a difference. First of all, it's in Lynbridge, a ten-minute walk up Lyn Way from Lynton; and it's Thai. But this is superior Thai food that has gained a host of enthusiasts. It's also well known for its Sunday roasts – and the owner brews his own beer, FatBelly Ale. Each year they host a Fat Belly Festival, which spans three evenings of music and merriment.

The Oak Room Lee Rd (opposite the town hall) ☎ 01598 753838 ⊘ theoakroomlynton. co.uk. Renowned for its tapas, though the regular menu of unusual Spanish dishes and a splendid seafood platter is good too. Popular with both locals and visitors.

The Picnic Box 1 Castle Hill ☎ 01598 753721. The best place in Lynton for a morning snack, lunch or tea. Or a take-away picnic, which you can phone ahead to order. Excellent sandwiches and cream teas, with a great selection of gluten-free and vegetarian choices.

The Vanilla Pod 10 Queen St, Lynton ☎ 01598 753706. The café is average but the meals – lunch or dinner – are beautifully cooked and very popular. The menu is varied and imaginative, with a Mediterranean bias.

Hollerday Hill & the Valley of Rocks

🌸 Croydecycle *Lynton & Lynmouth*; start: Lynton town hall; 2.4 miles (or via Lee Abbey, 6 miles); easy (mostly level but some ups & down); steep ascent from Lee Abbey

A track goes from beside the town hall and winds up to the site of Hollerday House, over the top of Hollerday Hill and on to the Valley of Rocks. Although there are easier approaches, Hollerday Hill and the scarcely visible remains of the house are a wonderfully peaceful place with great views so are worth the extra effort.

An easier walk, however, is to leave the track earlier and go straight ahead on a level path, parallel to the sea; you will soon see the first sign of the rocks, a monolith aptly known as The Castle. Other rocks, strewn around, have been given names: Rugged Jack, Devil's Cheesewring (see page 58 for an explanation for this strange name), Middle Gate and Chimney Rock. The path zigzags down to the flat valley bottom, where feral goats and Exmoor ponies graze. Head towards the roundabout opposite The Castle, and then follow the well-maintained path back to North Walk. This is a most beautiful path, cut into the side of the cliff, with benches where you can sit and admire the view. And what a view! Behind you are the rocks, in all shapes and sizes, and ahead is Lynmouth and the Bristol Channel.

The Castle (Castle Rock) can be climbed by a steadily rising path with superb views to the west and the sheer cliffs to the north bringing home the scale of this striking landscape. **Wringcliff Bay**, sandy at mid and low tide, is accessible down a steep path with some steps, and considered

12 LYNMOUTH

Tourist information: Exmoor National Park Centre, The Pavilion, The Esplanade, Lynmouth EX35 6EQ ✆ 01598 752509 ⌂ exmoor-nationalpark.gov.uk ⏱ 10.00–17.00 daily

Most people staying in Lynton walk down to Lynmouth and take the cliff railway (page 50) up. It's a very pleasant, steepish stroll down, the path lit by solar-powered lamps donated by different organisations. Lynmouth is clearly very much older than its partner, and very pretty with its harbour, cliffs and wooded hillsides.

Close to the Cliff Railway on The Esplanade in the western part of Lynmouth is **The Pavilion** and the **Exmoor National Park Centre**. The upstairs café here (page 57) is recommended for its tranquillity and views, and there's a well-stocked shop with maps and guides, displays of wildlife, webcams, an audiovisual presentation giving an overview of Exmoor, and a microscope with which you can study marine creatures collected on a guided tide-pooling excursion.

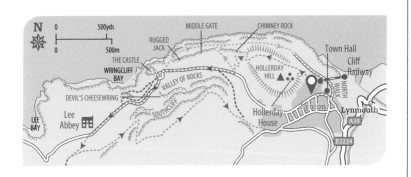

by a Lynton resident to be the area's best kept secret: 'Swimming is a challenge at low tide, but great at high tide for confident swimmers. And it gets the sun for most of the day.'

To make a longer walk, with the goal of an easier swim in Lee Bay or a light lunch or cream tea in a delightful garden, continue heading west until you see the impressive **Lee Abbey,** a Christian community centre and retreat. Beyond it, just before Lee Bay, is **Lee Abbey Tea Cottage** (✆ 01598 752621 ⏱ May–Sep 10.00–17.00), with tables set out in sun or shade in a tranquil garden. Return to Lynton on the track that zigzags up Southcliff on the south side of the road – a very steep climb, but you're rewarded with some splendid views.

"The river [Barle] section is particularly lovely with ever-changing scenery, and bits of history, ancient and relatively modern."

Continuing to the harbour, you can take a boat trip to Valley of Rocks and Lee Bay (Lynmouth Boat Trips ✆ 01598 753207) or continue strolling and buy an ice cream from one of the dozen or so outlets. The **Lynmouth Flood Memorial Hall**, on pedestrianised Lynmouth Street, houses two exhibitions. On the ground floor is the story of the famous lifeboat rescue of 1899 (see box, page 60), while the upper floor is given over to the great Lynmouth flood of 1952 when, after torrential rain on Exmoor, a wall of water carrying broken trees and boulders washed down the East and West Lyn rivers. It happened in the dead of night, with the electricity supply one of the first casualties, so all the terrified villagers could do was listen to the roar of the approaching torrent.

PERCY BYSSHE SHELLEY & LYNMOUTH

The poet Shelley was born in 1792. His father, a Whig MP and baronet, had high hopes that his son would follow him into parliament, sending him to Eton and Oxford. He was bullied at the former and expelled from the latter because of his rather too free distribution of a pamphlet he had written, *The Necessity of Atheism*. His next act of rebellion was to marry 16-year-old Harriet Westbrook, not so much because he loved her but because his father had told him that he would support any number of illegitimate children, but would not countenance an unsuitable marriage. He was 19. His father immediately stopped his allowance.

In 1812 the couple came to live in Lynmouth. Shelley described their approach to the village, down Countisbury Hill, as 'a fairy scene – little Lynmouth, then some thirty cottages, rose-clad and myrtle-clad, nestling at the foot of the hills. It was enough'. There is some debate as to where he lived, but most agree that it was at the cottage now named Shelley's Hotel.

Though he explored the area widely, he seems to have written little poetry in his new home, being more interested in disseminating information on radical politics. To this end he would row out from Lynmouth with leaflets sealed into bottles and even suspended from fire balloons. In this endeavour he was joined by a schoolmistress, Elizabeth Hitchener, and also co-opted his manservant Dan Hill to post extracts of Tom Paine's *Rights of Man* in Barnstaple, for which the poor man was arrested and imprisoned.

Life then became a little too hot in Lynmouth and the couple fled to Wales by boat, leaving a mass of unpaid debts and precious little poetry.

Subsequently Shelley fell in love with another 16-year-old, Mary, who went on to write *Frankenstein*. Harriet drowned herself in the Serpentine, and Mary and Percy married and moved to Italy where he was safe from prosecution, and where he started to write his best poetry. He died at sea aged 29 in 1822.

Many houses were destroyed and 34 people lost their lives. As with all major disasters, this has its own conspiracy theory – that at that time the government was experimenting with cloud seeding.

Some visitors only get as far as the main street, Riverside Road, and the pedestrianised Lynmouth Street. This is a pity since beyond the car park at the far end of town is the **Lynmouth Model Railway** (𝒫 01598 753330 ☉ Easter–Nov), built 'over several years' by Percy Howell from Yorkshire in the 1980s and now run by his son Leslie. It is all wonderfully busy and realistic, with the little trains running along a third of a mile of tracks, through tunnels and over bridges, and drawing up at stations. Beyond this, on Watersmeet Road, is a working pottery, **Ruffen Common** (☉ generally 10.00–17.00 daily), with a range of ceramics and some charming sculptures.

¶¶ FOOD & DRINK

7TheBistro 7 Watersmeet Rd 𝒫 01598 753302 ⊘ 7thebistro.com ☉ 18.30–late Tue–Sun.
A small, friendly bistro open only in the evenings and specialising in locally caught seafood, but with a good varied menu of other dishes. Always popular so book ahead.
The Esplanade Fish Bar 2 The Esplanade 𝒫 01598 753798 ☉ 11.45–21.00 daily.
A deservedly popular fish and chip shop facing the bay. Huge portions. Eat in or take away: beware seagulls if you eat outside!
Pavilion Dining Room First floor, Lynmouth Pavilion, The Esplanade (next to the cliff railway) 𝒫 01598 751064 ☉ 10.00–17.00 daily. Just the place for a light lunch or tea; uncrowded and with wonderful views over the harbour.

13 THE VALLEY OF ROCKS

The Valley of Rocks is accessible by car, but it's such a lovely walk that if you can it's well worth doing on foot from Lynton (see box, page 52). The valley, which would be unexceptional on Dartmoor, is quite extraordinary on Exmoor where the soft sandstone has left few sharp contours. The most likely explanation for these heaps and castles of rock is that this was once a river valley, the boulders being deposited during the Ice Age, before the river changed its course. Glaciation and weather erosion did the rest.

The place was already well known when R D Blackmore wrote *Lorna Doone* in the 1860s. The hero John Ridd goes there to consult a wise woman, noting that 'foreigners, who come and go without seeing much of Exmoor, have called [it] the "Valley of Rocks". The rocks already had their names: 'On the right hand is an upward crag, called by some "The Castle", easy enough to scale... Facing this, from the inland side and the elbow of the valley, a queer old pile of rock arises, bold behind one another, and quite enough to affright a man, if it only were ten times larger. This is called the "Devil's Cheesewring" or the "Devil's Cheese-knife" which mean the same thing, as our fathers were used to eat their cheese from a scoop; and perhaps in old time the upmost rock... was like to such an implement if Satan ate cheese untoasted.'

Watersmeet & the coastal path or via the Lyn to Rockford & beyond

✾ Croydecycle *Lynton & Lynmouth* ; start: Lynmouth, Tors Rd; 4 miles (or more); moderate with some steep climbs

This half-day walk takes in the full spectrum of Exmoor: village, river, tea room, moor, pub and coast. And it can be extended deep into Lorna Doone country. The 1½-mile path from Lynmouth to Watersmeet is both dramatic, up a deep, wooded gorge, and very easy, following the Lyn gently upstream. The path is often surfaced, so you can admire the woods and river, and look out for birds, without having to watch where you're going.

Start walking on the left side of the river; you'll cross to the right for a stretch, and then back again to Watersmeet, where the East Lyn River and Hoar Oak Water come together at the National Trust tea room at **Watersmeet House** (page 50).

From the lodge continue upstream, and you'll soon see the sign to Countisbury. Zigzag up the hill through a fairy-tale grove of stunted sessile oaks, all bent and twisted, and emerge on to the moor brightened by clumps of bell heather. Walk over the hill to the A39 and enjoy a pint or meal in the welcoming **Blue Ball Inn** or resist the temptation and cross the road to visit Countisbury Church, its pinnacled tower peeping above the horizon.

Ahead is **Foreland Point**, which adds another couple of miles to the walk if you want to stand on Devon's most northerly point, or you can take the coast path to the left and walk west back to the town. For Foreland Point set your sights on the radio mast, accessed by a grassy path, and admire the view before dropping down the other side. A path runs round the side of Foreland Point to the lighthouse, but it's precariously narrow, so not very inviting; best to take the lighthouse road there.

If you want to keep to the river and enjoy the best **wild swimming** on Exmoor, you have a choice from Watersmeet: take the path that follows the northern bank of the river or follow the stony track on the opposite side that leads through oak and beech woods. Either way,

CENTRAL EXMOOR

Central Exmoor is where you can find the real thing: high heather- and bracken-clad moorland and the patchwork green fields of the lowlands. On a sunny day it's sublime, in rain it can be utterly bleak but at least driving is easier on the high, open-view lanes. With Badgworthy Water flowing from its source north of Simonsbath, this is the landscape described in *Lorna Doone*; it gives walkers and mountain bikers that

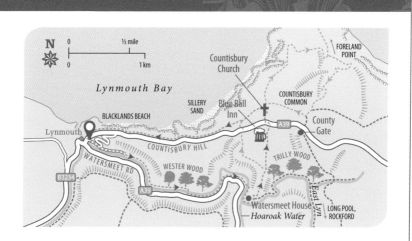

it's 1½ miles to the hamlet of **Rockford** and the Rockford Inn, with **Long Pool**, which is marked on the Croydecycle map, roughly a mile from Watersmeet. Joanna Griffin describes this as 'the absolute pinnacle of wild swimming'. Follow the river along the south bank upstream from the National Trust tea room: a short steep path to the left, shortly after Ash Bridge, leads to the pool. 'Long Pool is easy to miss, being below the main footpath, but this, along with the moss-covered banks, gives it a special secluded feel,' says Joanna. 'It's a bit of a scramble over rather slippery rocks to get in but once you're in there is a lovely deep stretch, long enough for a good swim upstream towards the waterfall. The current can be strong here, providing an endless-pool effect for stronger swimmers, or you can let it sweep you back downstream to shallower water.'

From Rockford you can take the quiet lanes back to Hillford Bridge and down Hoaroak Water to Watersmeet.

perfect combination of high moor and sheltered combes. And in the wooded valleys that enfold the East Lyn River as it meanders west to Lynmouth, you would scarcely know you were in Exmoor.

DOONE COUNTRY

From Watersmeet the lovely East Lyn River draws you towards Brendon and on into Somerset where it becomes Oare Water. This is a seductive region of tea shops, pubs, medieval bridges – and Lorna Doone.

Further along the road or path from Rockford is Brendon, another small village with a welcoming pub, the **Staghunter's Inn** (📞 01598

A DARK & STORMY NIGHT

Janice Booth

'Vessel in distress,' reported a message telegraphed from Porlock Weir to Lynmouth Post Office. A force-eight gale had raged all day in the Bristol Channel and by evening Lynmouth's lower streets were awash. Further along the coast, off Gore Point near Porlock, the three-masted barque *Forrest Hall* was tossing helplessly, held only by her anchors; she'd been on tow from Bristol to Liverpool when her tug suffered damage and had to abandon her to the storm. The nearest lifeboat, at Watchet, could not launch in the heavy seas, and the telegram requested assistance from the Lynmouth lifeboat. This was in January 1899, when lifeboats were rowed manually and ships could go to their graves in the time that it took for help to arrive. A maroon was fired to summon the lifeboat's crew. The doors of the lifeboat shed were opened but it was clear that the boat – the 3½-ton *Louisa* – had no hope of launching into the churning sea. It was decided to haul her the 13 miles overland to Porlock Weir, and to attempt

a launch from there. Horses were brought – with extra ones for the steep two-mile climb up Countisbury Hill – and ropes were attached to the trailer that bore the lifeboat. Torches and flares were lit. From every home, heedless of weather and darkness, villagers came to help with the preparations, and within an hour of the telegram's arrival all was set. It seemed barely possible, but everyone agreed: 'We'll try'. On her trailer, the *Louisa* weighed ten tons. Slowly and laboriously, men and horses together hauled her up the hill. At the summit some men, exhausted, returned home; 20 remained to see her across the moor in the teeth of the storm. Rain and wind extinguished the torches, which had to be continually re-lit. Ropes were slippery and hard to grip. At one point a wheel came off; the boat had to be lifted manually so it could be replaced. One lane was too narrow for the trailer, so the *Louisa* was lowered on to wooden skids and dragged through while the trailer took a longer route; when they met again the boat

741222), highly praised for its excellent food, atmosphere, and as a base for walkers. From here an inviting path runs along the bottom of a steep escarpment into Somerset and then back along the top to Brendon.

"If you sit outside at the Lorna Doone Inn your cream tea will be shared by bold wild birds."

You are now in Lorna Doone country. In **Malmsmead**, at the **Lorna Doone Inn** (✆ 01598 741450) if you sit outside, your cream tea will be shared by bold wild birds. Near the packhorse bridge over Badgworthy Water, which marks the boundary with Somerset, is **Lorna Doone Farm**. A walk to the legendary Doone hideout (see box, page 64) starts from here.

---

was heaved back up. A small group went ahead with picks and spades to widen the narrow lane at Culbone.

Next came the notorious Porlock Hill, a dizzily steep descent needing all available man- and horsepower to prevent the whole thing from hurtling downwards to destruction. At the bottom a garden wall had to be demolished – the lady householder, who had never seen a lifeboat before, enthusiastically joined in the work. Eventually, ten hours after leaving Lynmouth, the *Louisa* was dragged on to the beach at Porlock Weir.

Refusing to rest, the 13 lifeboatmen clambered aboard as helpers pushed the boat into the battering waves. After rowing for about an hour they located the *Forrest Hall*, whose anchors had dragged but held firm. To evacuate her frightened 19-man crew in so wild a sea would have risked lives; she seemed in no immediate danger so the *Louisa* simply stood by. As day broke the barque was drifting alarmingly close

to shore but her tug returned in the nick of time. Some of the lifeboat crew clambered aboard and attached her tow-lines; the *Louisa* then accompanied her, still pounded by the storm, as she was towed to a place of safety on the Welsh coast. There the men had a meal and a hearty sleep before rowing back to Lynmouth – and a heroes' welcome – the following day.

No human lives were lost but, sadly, four of the horses that had hauled the boat died from their exertions. The cost of the rescue, including repairs to damaged roads and gardens, was £118.17s.6d, of which the *Forrest Hall's* owners paid £75. Members of the *Louisa's* crew each received £5 from local funds and a silver watch from a wealthy local resident. You can find more details of this extraordinary story of courage and determination in the exhibition at Lynmouth and the little museum in Porlock Weir where there's the saying: 'If it's not us, then it's nobody. And it's never not nobody, not in the lifeboat service.'

14 Oare

For Lorna Doone fans the church of St Mary is a must-see – it's where the dastardly Carver Doone shot Lorna through a small window on the south side on her wedding day. The window in question is now identified for visitors. R D Blackmore's grandfather was rector of St Mary's from 1809 to 1842 so the author of *Lorna Doone* knew the place well. Setting that aside, it's a church with lots of interest. Note the box pews. The one for the squire has seats round three sides so he and his family could be fenced off from his labourers, and in a position to ignore the vicar if so inclined.

"It's where the dastardly Carver Doone shot Lorna through a small window on her wedding day."

Note also the Ten Commandments, painted in the 18th century on wooden boards at the entrance to the inner chancel. Shortening of 'the' to 'ye' is common, but here we have 'yt' for 'that'. A head held between two hands forms the unusual piscina. This is thought to be St Decuman, who was briefly separated from his head but went on to inspire the building of the church dedicated to him in Watchet. What he is doing in Oare is unclear.

LORNA DOONE: FACT & FICTION

Janice Booth

For a fictional heroine, Lorna Doone has had a surprisingly powerful effect on Exmoor tourism. Little can her creator R D Blackmore have known, as she flowed from his pen, that 21st-century tourists would be seeking out her home and exclaiming over her dramatic life. Her romantic tale is so intertwined with factual places and characters that it's hard to know where imagination takes over from truth. Some of the characters apparently did exist in some form, but not contemporaneously with the story, so Blackmore will have heard of them and woven them into his plot. What is undeniably true is that he caught just the right mixture of love, heroism, villainy and derring-do for his era and the book has remained consistently popular, receiving praise from (among others) Thomas Hardy, Robert Louis Stevenson and Gerard Manley Hopkins.

In his preface to the book in 1869, Blackmore writes:

This work is called a 'romance', because the incidents, characters, time, and scenery are alike romantic. And in shaping this old tale, the Writer neither dares, nor desires, to claim for it the dignity, or cumber it with the difficulty, of an historic novel.

A modern feature of the church is the beautiful carved buzzard lectern created by the sculptor Mike Leach to replace the traditional eagle lectern, which was stolen.

From Oare, walkers heading up Clannel Combe to the A39 for the Quantock Heritage Bus will look in dismay at the near vertical hill they need to climb. Cyclists and drivers will continue east along a delightfully scenic lane that crosses Robber's Bridge (another Doone reference) before climbing up to the main road in a series of hairpin bends.

15 SIMONSBATH & THE RIVER BARLE

Why Simon's Bath? No one knows, though legend has it that a deep pool in the Barle some 100 yards above the bridge was the bathing place of an outlaw, Simon, terror of Exmoor.

Penguin Guide to Somerset, 1939

Despite its history of being the place where James Boevey enclosed a hundred acres of moorland for the first Exmoor farm, **Simonsbath**

The fictional Lorna was kidnapped from a noble family, as a child, by the dastardly Doone outlaws of Exmoor. The Doones (or Dounes) seem to stem from fact: in the 17th century such a family (possibly Scottish miscreants who had fled south to escape the law) did live in the area around Badgworthy Water and Hoccombe Combe, and terrorised the inhabitants. Tales of their exploits existed locally and Blackmore, writing *Lorna Doone* in the late 1860s, will have heard them.

Fair Lorna's lover was (true to romantic tradition) honest local farmer John Ridd; a boy of this name existed and went to school in Tiverton, as did Blackmore, but there any record of him ends. In the novel, the Doones murdered his father when he was 12. Later, Blackmore has him stray into Doone country when following a stream in search of loach, where he meets the young Lorna.

As adults they meet again and fall in love. Naturally, and unsurprisingly given that a paperback version of the book today runs to 627 pages and 75 chapters, the course of their love does not flow smoothly: Lorna doesn't get into her wedding gown until page 613 – and then a shot rings out as Carver Doone fires his carbine at her through the window of Oare Church, where she and John have just exchanged their marriage vows.

To say any more would, of course, ruin the suspense of the ending.

Doone Valley walk

❋ OS Explorer map OL9 or Croydecycle *Lynton, Lynmouth & Doone Valley*; start: Malmsmead car park; 6 miles or 2½ miles; easy to moderate, may be boggy underfoot

Two rivers, Badgworthy (pronounced Badgery) Water and Oare Water, meet at Malmsmead to become the East Lyn. A path runs south along Badgworthy Water through the Doone Valley to Hoccombe Combe and the remains of a medieval village, thought to be the inspiration for Doone Glen. En route it passes the memorial stone to R D Blackmore. It's a lovely circular walk, taking around three hours, and combining a level riverside section through oak woods, to high moorland which, in the summer, is purple with heather.

A shorter circuit brings you to **Cloud Farm** and its tea rooms (☉ summer & winter, all day), and then along footpaths to Oare or back to Malmsmead.

Park in the long-stay car park in Malmsmead and walk back to the village and up the hill straight ahead to the start of the bridleway on your left, signposted Badgworthy Valley. Follow this track and then a grassy path next to the wire fence. Drop down to the river and the little footbridge to Cloud Farm Tea Room and Oare.

For the Doone Valley, keep the river on your left. With its deep pools and fast-flowing sections it fits the description in the book where the boy John Rudd went fishing for loach. Soon after the Cloud Farm footbridge you'll come to the **Blackmore Memorial Stone** on your right, erected for the centenary of the book's publication. Passing through a gate into Badgworthy Wood, you cross over Yealscombe Water, and come to the loveliest part of the walk with fern and moss-covered oak trees flanking the river. Shortly before the Lankcombe Water footbridge the path forks. Ignore the right-hand fork and continue beside the river and over the footbridge, through woods as the path gently rises to meet open moor. This is the site of the **medieval village** – you can see the remains of stone walls – and the legendary Doone Glen.

(pronounced Simmonsbath) is a relatively modern settlement that grew up at the crossroads of two tracks. It's now popular as a walking base and for the annual **Simonsbath Festival** (⊘ simonsbathfestival.org.uk), which runs for six weeks each year from early May and offers a daily programme of events varying from walks to music and readings by local authors. For meals you have the **Exmoor Forest Inn** (⊘ 01643 831341) and there's a convenient car park for the many walks to be enjoyed in the area, most notably along the **River Barle**. Once a month the water-powered Simonsbath sawmill is open to the public (usually the third Monday but check ⊘ simonsbathsawmill.org.uk).

At the three-way signpost follow the contour of the hill around to the right, away from the river, then uphill to cross a small stream. Pause and enjoy the view, then continue uphill to pass through the metal gate and follow a wide track down to Lankcombe Ford. Bear right up to the main track and Malmsmead is signposted. When the track curves round to the right you can take the shorter, scenic route along the less distinct path to the left, heading for distant trees. This will rejoin the main track, which leads you back to the road. Turn right to walk downhill to Malmsmead and some well-earned refreshment.

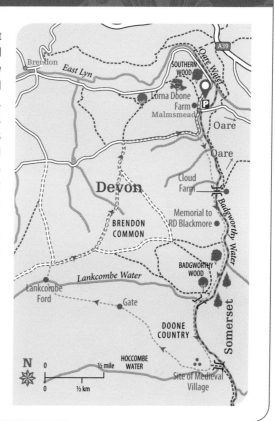

SOUTHERN EXMOOR

The rivers Barle and Exe flow through attractive villages in the southern section of the moor, with Exmoor's ancient clapper bridge, Tarr Steps, drawing a host of visitors in the summer.

16 WITHYPOOL

This village ticks all the boxes. It has a thatched pub brimming with literary, artistic and historical associations, an excellent post office/village shop (☉ daily) that sells everything you might need, including

CHURCHES

Churches are always worth investigating. They contain some of the richest collections of rural art in the country and Exmoor's churches are no exception to this.

1 Culbone, the smallest parish church in England. 2 A medieval stained-glass window at Winsford. 3 St Mary's church at Oare, where Lorna Doone was shot on her wedding day. 4 The decorative lychgate at Dulverton. 5 A poppyhead bench carving in Combe Martin shows the town's agricultural heritage. 6 Selworthy Church is traditionally limewashed. 7 The interior of Wootton Courtenay's distinctive church.

River Barle, mine & moor

✻ OS Explorer map 24; start: Simonsbath car park ♀ SS77383941; 6.7 miles; moderately easy with no steep ups & downs; option for wild swimming in the river

O ne of Exmoor's most popular inland walks, this combines a riverside stroll in one direction and a high-level return with good views. The river section is particularly lovely, with ever-changing scenery and bits of history, ancient and relatively modern. The more recent story belongs to Wheal Eliza, a copper mine that was one of the projects of the Knight family. From 1845 to 1854 it mined copper, and when this ran out it switched to iron for three years before being abandoned. A year later the mine was in the news when little Anna Maria Burgess was killed by her father and her body hidden in the one of the mine shafts. He was brought to justice and hanged.

The next landmark is **Cow Castle**, an Iron-Age hillfort built around 3,000 years ago; from a high point on the walk you can see the enclosing ramparts. The river here has some lovely deep pools, ideal for wild swimming.

After skirting some conifers, you leave the good bridle path that continues to Withypool and turn back towards Picked Stones Farm (pronounced pickéd) and Simonsbath over rather bleak, heather-free moorland and conifer plantations.

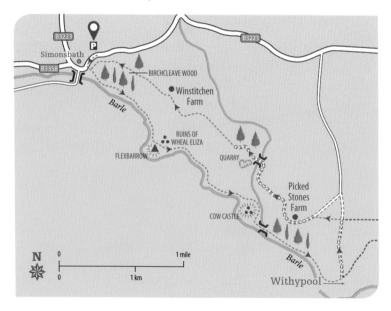

maps and walking guides, an above-average tea room, benches in the sun, and some historic Shell petrol pumps looking like the remnants of our civilisation in a post-apocalypse movie.

A footpath runs from the east side of the village along the banks of the River Barle to Tarr Steps, a four-mile walk.

The Royal Oak dates from the 17th century and has hosted R D Blackmore, who supposedly wrote part of *Lorna Doone* in its bar, and the equestrian artist Sir Alfred Munnings who had a studio in the garret. The owner was the inspiration for Ian Fleming's M, and finally General Eisenhower planned the Normandy Invasion while staying here.

17 EXFORD

The Exe, a mere stream at Simonsbath, has gathered strength from two tributaries and is a proper river by the time it reaches Exford, giving the village much of its charm. It is seriously picturesque with its huge village green and 15th-century White Horse Inn dripping with Virginia creeper (page 78), and is quite a bustling village with a post office, a good range of shops and a few tea rooms (page 75). It is also the home of Exmoor's **blueberry farm**, Sharcott Farm, which offers pick-your-own blueberries in August and September (𝒶 exmoorblueberries.co.uk).

Held in mid-August is the **Exford Show**, with Exmoor ponies and equestrian events to the fore, along with parades of hounds, classes for Exmoor breeds of sheep and stands selling Exmoor crafts and produce. Everything, in fact, to showcase the Exmoor way of life.

18 WINSFORD

Winsford is often described as one of Exmoor's prettiest villages. Its location is idyllic, the Royal Oak pub is chocolate-box charming, and there's a general store and post office next to it. See if you can find all Winsford's eight bridges. Or maybe it's six. Or five – I've read various claims. Both the Exe and the Winn flow through the village.

The **church**, set above the town, is interesting for its 14th-century stained-glass window. It is said to be the oldest in Devon, but other churches have also made the same claim. Occupying just one section in the otherwise clear-glass eastern window, it shows a feisty boy Jesus dressed in yellow trousers, sitting astride Mary's shoulder. He is thrusting a bunch of flowers towards his care-worn mother. It's a vigorous and charming portrayal that needs binoculars or a zoom lens to be seen properly.

Withypool to the medieval Landacre Bridge & Sherdon Hutch

❄ OS Explorer map OL9; start: Withypool car park; 4–6 miles; easy to moderate

If you opt for a there-and-back walk, this is a pleasant, mostly level four-mile stroll: at first along the River Barle, and then up on to bleak moorland, to one of Exmoor's oldest bridges, Landacre. It can be extended to about six miles if you come back via the Two Moors Way or opt to go upriver to Sherdon Hutch for a swim.

The path to Landacre is signposted at the Withypool bridge. It follows the river for nearly a mile, sometimes boggy underfoot and crossing several stiles until the path leaves the river and heads uphill to Brightworthy Farm. The public right of way takes you through the farm and uphill through open moorland (Withypool Common) from where you can see **Landacre Bridge** (sometimes called Lanacre, which gives a clue to its pronunciation). When you reach a road turn right and the River Barle is a short distance away. The five-arched bridge is impressive, especially when you consider that it has stood here since the 14th century or thereabouts. The riverbanks are a popular picnic spot.

If you have your swim things with you and it's a sunny day, turn left rather than right when you reach the road above the bridge. You are heading towards Sherdon Hutch ('hutch' is a local word for sluicegate) at the confluence of the Barle and Sherdon Water, which is popular for wild swimming. After about a quarter-mile walking uphill, look for a rough track on your right and

19 TARR STEPS

Perhaps Exmoor's best-known inland attraction, this is a beautifully preserved clapper bridge over the River Barle. Some say it's over a thousand years old but it's more likely to date from the 13th century. Either way, the feat of building it out of giant slabs of stone, which were brought in from a considerable distance, is remarkable. Some slabs are over six feet long and weigh more than a ton. Despite their size they are periodically washed away after heavy rain swells the river. All have been numbered so they can be reassembled correctly.

There's a spacious car park some way above the river, but there's disabled parking near the bridge, next to **Tarr Farm** with its irresistible teas and walkers' menu (page 78). Tarr Steps is perfect for a family picnic, though it can get very crowded in the summer. Children and dogs love the paddling, and there are several deep pools where you can get fully immersed if you wish. Be cautious about sunbathing on

follow it for a bit under half a mile, keeping your eye out for a path leading down to the river. There are deep pools just below the confluence. Return the way you came.

To return to Withypool you can either retrace your steps or, energetically, take the lane uphill for a bit under a mile to the junction with the Two Moors Way. Turn right here and follow the broad track until it becomes Kitridge Lane (an old droving road), which brings you back to your car. Watch out for the signposted footpath to Withypool which takes you a more direct route than the lane.

the stones, however – that's the Devil's prerogative. Legend has it that he built the bridge, so was understandably peeved when mere mortals tried to use it. The locals asked the vicar to help; he prudently sent a cat across first to test the waters, so to speak, but it disappeared in a puff of smoke. Undaunted, the reverend set out himself and after a heated argument the Devil agreed to let people use the bridge. Except when he wants to sunbathe.

There's an easy circular walk up one side of the river and back the other side, and a longer, more varied one described in the box on page 72. For the energetic there's a pleasant eight-mile walk along the right-hand (eastern) bank of the river to Withypool, where you can enjoy a snack before picking up the Two Moors Way back towards Tarr Steps, turning left towards the river at the T-junction at Parsonage Farm. This, and the walk to Dulverton (see box, page 118), are shown on the Croydecycle map *Dulverton & Tarr Steps*.

20 HAWKRIDGE

Hawkridge is one of those tiny, high (nearly 1,000 feet) and isolated communities that still exist in Exmoor. It has a population of around 40, there are just ten houses in the village and the community spirit is strongly evident in the **Hawkridge Revel and Gymkhana**, which has been run on August Bank Holiday for nearly 75 years. They get up to all sorts of things – dog show, mounted games, fancy dress – and stalls selling various goodies including plants 'which will probably survive anywhere in the UK'.

The squat **church of St Giles** seems to be hunkered down against the elements, but overlooks a glorious view of the moors. Inside, the visitors' book is full of thanks from tired walkers for keeping it open (Hawkridge lies on the Two Moors Way). There's a Norman font, but the most notable feature is the stone coffin lid which was found in the

---

Tarr Steps circular walk

❄ Croydecycle *Dulverton & Tarr Steps*; start: Tarr Steps car park ♥ SS872323; 2 miles or 4½ miles; easy

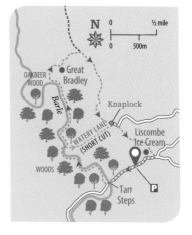

This is such a lovely area for walking, it makes sense to spend some time here. An hour's stroll takes you along the right (eastern) bank of the Barle, upriver (the car park side), through ancient woods, then up Watery Lane (more of a path than a lane) to Knaplock where you turn right. Follow the signs to Liscombe, rather than Tarr Steps, and you will join the lane to the car park, but not before visiting Liscombe Farm Ice Cream Parlour (see opposite).

If you want to extend the walk, just keep going upriver, instead of turning off for Watery Lane, to a bridleway signposted Winsford Hill and walk uphill, briefly joining the lane that serves the Great Bradley Estate. After crossing a cattle grid you leave the lane, bearing right to walk up a grassy track. Follow signs to Knaplock, and then to Tarr Steps via Liscombe, which will bring you out above the car park.

wall behind the pulpit in 1877. It has inscriptions in Norman French and Latin, and was probably for William de Plessy, Lord of the Manor, who died in 1274.

Hawkridge is in the same parish as Tarr Steps, and the Devil, who caused so many problems to the early users of his bridge, also wreaked havoc with the masons who built the church of St Giles, cutting their apron strings as they carried the stones for the church across the River Barle.

If you're planning to drive to Tarr Steps from Hawkridge, be warned: the river can be too deep for an ordinary saloon car to cross the ford, and there is no parking on the west side of the river. It's a lovely walk down there from Hawkridge, however, and you can make it a circular walk by taking the Two Moors Way there and coming back via the lane.

BEYOND TARR STEPS
Motorists driving towards Winsford tend to pass through this bleak area unseeingly, but there are some surprises here if you know where to stop.

Liscombe Farm Ice Cream Parlour
07496 557145 from Easter 11.00–17.00 Sat–Thu

Passing the ice-cream sign you might think this is an ordinary parlour. It's not, it's unique. In 2013 Zoe and Ollie Rose sold their farm in Dorset to move to Exmoor for their children's sake. Zoe describes them as 'feral' and indeed their childhood sounds close to Enid Blyton perfection. The dairy side of the farm consists of 70 or so Brown Swiss cows ('they are tough enough to cope with the Exmoor climate', Zoe told me. 'Friesians hate it here.'). The other advantage of these beautiful cows is their rich, creamy milk – ideal for ice cream. Out of a total of 40 flavours, 24 are on offer at a time, and the recipe used is gelato, which is softer and creamier than regular ice cream. And the unique part? You can watch the cows being milked by robot through a huge glass window while enjoying your ice cream. From the spacious barn where they spend the cold, wet months, the cows wander in with food on their minds: cow cake, tastier than their regular fodder. Each wears an identifying tag on its collar so the robot recognises the individual cow and attaches the clusters to its udder. The cow munches, the milk travels up transparent tubes to a holding tank, and when the milk is finished and the cow has had its treat it rejoins the herd. It brings a whole new dimension to enjoying an ice cream.

It's fascinating to watch, and of course enthralling for children who are more used to seeing milk in a plastic bottle on a supermarket shelf. The milk not used for ice cream is sold to a milk dealer, but there are plans to sell it themselves locally.

In addition to the ever-fascinating view of the 'cow to cone' process and the ice cream itself, there is also a spacious tea room for cream teas.

21 WINSFORD HILL & THE CARATACUS STONE

Above Liscombe, under a little shelter on the western flank of **Winsford Hill** (SS88963355), is an inscribed standing stone, known as the **Caratacus Stone**; somewhat unimpressive to look at but, like so many stones and monuments on Exmoor, with an interesting story connected to it (see box, below).

THE CARATACUS STONE

Janice Booth

Caratacus was a powerful 1st-century British chieftain of the Catuvellauni tribe and a considerable irritation to the Romans, against whom he waged guerrilla and open warfare for almost a decade. The rough weathered megalith on Winsford Hill probably dates from the 6th century, and remnants of words carved on it (CARAACI or CARATACI NEPVS) suggest that it's a memorial to someone claiming to be descended from his family.

The stone was first mentioned in 1219, in *A Perambulation of the Royal Forest of Exmoor*. Its brick shelter was erected in 1906 and it was declared a scheduled monument in 1925.

Devon has a handful of other inscribed memorial stones from roughly the same period; apart from those in Yealmpton and Lustleigh churchyards and the Lundy cemetery they are on private land. The Caratacus stone is the only one known in Somerset, and the only one with a historically recognisable name.

During around AD43–51 Caratacus (or Caractacus: the Roman historian Tacitus used both spellings) resisted the Roman invasion fiercely across the south of England, using the terrain to his advantage when possible. But eventually Rome proved too strong. After his final defeat in battle he fled north to what is now Yorkshire, seeking sanctuary from the powerful Queen Cartimandua of the Brigantes; but she sneakily handed him over to the Romans. With his brothers, wife and daughter (who had been captured earlier) he was taken to Rome in chains as a trophy of war, to be paraded triumphally before the populace. Facing trial and then almost certain death, in recognition of his status he was first allowed to plead his case to the emperor Claudius. To loosely paraphrase translations from the *Annals* of Tacitus:

Winsford Hill, looked after by the National Trust, is popular with walkers and is the highest place in this part of Exmoor. On a clear day you can pick out the tors of Dartmoor.

🍴 FOOD & DRINK

Exford Bridge Tea Rooms Chapel St ✆ 01643 831304. The name is misleading – this excellent place serves breakfast from 08.30, and light lunches as well as yummy teas. It's licensed so you can enjoy a beer or cider with your meal, and it also does packed lunches. Sit by a snug fire in the winter or out in the garden in the summer. See ad, page 131.
The Royal Oak Winsford ✆ 01643 851455 🖱 royaloakexmoor.co.uk. Once a 12th-century farmhouse, it retains its charm while providing very good meals. There are at least four internal dining areas here – they can probably seat 120 people – and most are dog friendly. The menu is classic pub fare and reasonably priced.

... Had my success [in battle] been as great as my nobility and fortune, I would have come to this city as a friend rather than a captive ... I had horses, men, arms, and wealth: is it surprising that I was unwilling to lose them? If you wish to command the world, should the world necessarily accept its enslavement readily? Had I been brought here today as one who had surrendered instantly, neither my fortune nor your achievement would have merited fame. Punish me, and you send me to oblivion. But if you spare me, I shall stand as an eternal example of your clemency.

His speech was so well judged, eloquent and persuasive that Claudius relented: Caratacus and his family were allowed to remain in Rome and live freely. He later commented wryly that, seeing Rome's many fine possessions, he wondered why they should also covet Britain's poor tents.

Caratacus's name has cropped up in various literary works over the past four centuries or so, also in music (a cantata by Elgar) and even *The Goon Show* (remember Caractacus Seagoon?). Shakespeare's *Cymbeline* is said to be based loosely on the reign of his father, Cunobelinus.

Various artists, too, have depicted him making his speech to Claudius; and in William Blake's *Visionary Heads* illustrations he appears as a peppery old man with a high collar and a splendid corkscrew moustache. Perhaps he would have preferred the lonely rough-hewn stone memorial on Winsford Hill.

"Exmoor ponies all look remarkably similar –
short and hairy, with brown bodies that are
dark on top and lighter underneath and a
characteristic mealy muzzle."

Tarr Farm Inn Tarr Steps 🖉 01643 851507 🖉 tarrfarm.co.uk. A splendid inn serving outstanding food in a lovely location. What more could you want? Its large garden is ideal for a relaxed lunch or cream tea after a long walk, while it's more formal in the evenings for the award-winning à la carte menu. The steak here, from Red Ruby cattle raised and slaughtered on their own farm, was described by a friend as the best he'd ever had, and their menu is accompanied by a choice of over 100 different wines.

White Horse Inn Exford 🖉 08721 077077 🖉 exmoor-whitehorse.co.uk. Excellent food in cosy surroundings, including an indulgent five-course dinner. Log fires in cold weather and, they claim, the finest single malt whisky collection in the South West. B&B available.

Withypool Tea Rooms 🖉 01643 831178 ⊙ spring/summer 10.00–17.00 daily. Cream teas, cakes, savoury pastries, light lunches as well as really good coffee and a terrific variety of teas.

PORLOCK & AREA

Back to the coast and this very agreeable small town, which makes an excellent base for exploring northeast Exmoor. **Walkers** are spoiled for choice, with coastal walks and inland trails through Horner Woods and up Dunkery Beacon, which has, in August, the best purple-heather views in Exmoor. *Porlock Walks* by Gill and Alistair Campbell, contributors to this book, has detailed descriptions of 12 local walks; guided Heritage Walks are held twice monthly. Croydecycle's maps *Porlock*, *Horner* & *Dunkery*, and *Minehead*, *Dunster*, *Selworthy* have the region well covered. All booklets and maps are available from the very good tourist information centre (page 80).

"Walkers are spoiled for choice, with coastal walks and inland trails through Horner Woods."

The only downside, however, is that the number 300 bus between Minehead and Lynmouth only currently runs twice a day for a couple of months in the summer (page 16), and its future is uncertain. So linear walks using the bus need careful planning.

Strong cyclists, if they can cope with Porlock Hill, have some lovely villages and quiet lanes to enjoy. Bicycles may be hired from **Exmoor Adventures** (page 17) or **Porlock Pedals** (🖉 07866 330321), in the Old Tannery Courtyard near D J Miles & Co.

If you are approaching or leaving Porlock via Porlock Hill, look out for the **Whit Stones** (white stones), at 📍 SS8532846255, just past a lane forking off to the left if coming from Porlock. There are two parking

PORLOCK HILL

Alistair Campbell

In 1794 it was recorded that there was 'no road suitable for carriages' beyond Porlock, and the poet Robert Southey wrote that local people considered it 'the end of the world'.

Eighteen years later the track up the hill was still so poorly kept that the inhabitants of Porlock Parish were summoned to court and fined for failing to maintain a good road. A man was employed to do the work and in 1843 the first stagecoach, from Lynton, made it down to Porlock.

About this time Mr Blaithwaite, a local estate owner, saw an opportunity to build a toll road further west. The 4½-mile Toll Road, with a maximum gradient of just one in 14, is longer and much less steep than the public road, the A39. At first it wasn't popular, drivers preferring to save money by coaxing their horses up the main road.

These days the A39 twists and bends its way up Porlock Hill, climbing 1,300 feet in under two miles. It is the steepest main road in England, so steep that for many years motor cars were not powerful enough to climb the one in four (25%) gradients and negotiate the hairpin bends. The Toll Road was the only alternative and remained popular until long after World War I.

In 1900 a rally driver, Mr S F Edge, was the first to drive a car up Porlock Hill to win a £50 bet – more than £5,000 today. The first motorcycle climbed the hill in 1909 but the first charabanc motor coach did not make it up until 1916.

As a child, I was driven up this hill annually by my father when going on holiday. As we approached, everyone became a little apprehensive and my grandmother handed out barley-sugars to calm our nerves!

Even today, the drive up or down is challenging. Caravans and lorries are told to seek an alternative route and cyclists are advised to dismount. Car drivers are probably not reassured by signs at the top telling of the two escape roads, designed to minimise damage should you lose control.

areas on the right – stop at the second one, cross the road and take the little path through the heather. You should soon come to the two standing stones – actually leaning so much they are almost lying, rather than standing. But that's not surprising when you consider they are the result of a hurling match between the Devil (yes, him again) and St Dubricius. Standing on the northern point of Bossington Beach, they flung their stones as far as they could. The saint's landed just a few feet further, he won the contest, and the Devil has been only spasmodically tiresome ever since. That northern point is now called Hurlstone.

Or, if you prefer, they are late Neolithic standing stones, and possibly remnants of a burial chamber.

22 PORLOCK

Tourist information: The Old School, West End, High St, TA24 8QD ✆ 01643 863150
🖥 porlock.co.uk ⊙ summer 10.00–12.30 & 14.00–17.00 Mon–Fri, 10.00–17.00 Sat,
10.00–13.00 Sun, winter 10.00–12.30 daily

Porlock, along with Lynmouth and Lynton, is one of the three most populated parishes on Exmoor. It combines its villagey feel with wonderful rural surroundings, yet provides all the amenities that visitors need: some delightful cottages and gardens, interesting shops and good restaurants, pubs and tea shops. The poet Robert Southey loved it, writing to his brother: 'If only beauty of landscape were to influence me in choice of residence, I should at once fix on Porlock.'

The town is tightly contained along its High Street where almost every business provides something desirable, whether cream teas, specialist cheeses, antiquarian books, or paintings and crafts. Set back from the main street in Vale Yard is the factory and shop of **D J Miles & Co Ltd** (🖥 djmiles.co.uk), a family firm well known for their specialist teas and coffees; here the coffee is roasted, ground, blended – and sold, together with tea, chocolate and a whole lot of other temptations. They are now running occasional Roastery Tours – check the website for dates.

"The town is tightly contained along its High Street where almost every business provides something desirable."

Near the church, **The Big Cheese** has a popular café as well as a wide selection of local cheeses, preserves, chutney and cider, and further down the road is **Mrs Jackson's Victorian Tea Rooms**, one of several offering cream teas, though this feels a little bit more special: bone china and a huge array of home-baked cakes and treats, including crumpets. And they close at 17.00 – so you don't have to rush.

On the High Street towards Doverhay is something completely different: **Squire**. Ostensibly a pet shop, the place is crammed with antler creations and vintage entertainments; try the one-armed bandit. And then you meet the owner, Richard. Think Brian Blessed without a beard and multiply tenfold, and you'll be somewhat prepared for Richard.

Art is well represented, with several art and craft galleries including the upmarket **Churchgate Gallery**, which represents 30 artists from across the country and publishes its own art books.

The truncated steeple of the **church** provides a handy landmark; legend has it that the top of the steeple landed up on Culbone, possibly with the help of a giant, but a storm in the 1700s was probably responsible. It is dedicated to St Dubricius, an obscure Welsh saint credited with the crowning of Alfred the Great as king of England, and is full of interest. There are two exceptional monuments, one to John, Lord Harington, who fought for Henry V at the Battle of Agincourt, providing 86 archers and 29 lancers. He died a year later, presumably of his wounds. His wife Elizabeth lies by his side, with her feet on a strange, cloven-hoofed animal. The other effigy is a knight, crossed-legged to show that he fought in the Crusades, dating from the end of the 13th century. What strikes the observer of these monuments, first with shock, then with curiosity, is the quantity and age of the graffiti scratched into the soft alabaster. Nothing is sacrosanct – Elizabeth's face is covered in initials. Who would have defaced the tomb in this way back in the 17th century when most of the population was illiterate? We'll never know.

"What strikes the observer, first with shock, then with curiosity, is the quantity and age of the graffiti."

The clock at the western end of the nave possibly dates from around 1450, but the oldest object in the church is the fragment of a pre-Norman cross set in the wall of the south aisle.

Beside the church, a stroll up Parsons Street to the area called Hawkcombe brings you to some attractive old cottages; carry on and you'll come to the woods of Hawk Combe. Here the path follows Hawkcombe Water up to Hawkcombe Head, which is open moorland with plenty of walking opportunities.

The oldest secular building in Porlock is the delightful **Dovery Manor**, at the eastern end of the town. This small 15th-century manor is home to the local museum (doverymanormuseum.org.uk May–Sep 10.00–17.00 Mon–Fri, 10.30–16.30 Sat) and is a lovely example of the architecture of the time. Its exhibits relate mostly to Porlock and

DID YOU KNOW?

A garderobe, the forerunner to a wardrobe, was an early lavatory built into upper-class houses and castles. The excrement, etc dropped down a shaft into a moat or garden. There's a fine example of one at Dovery Manor Museum in Porlock, complete with a spike to hold the dock leaves that served as loo paper. Here it's explained that clothes were hung there to ward off moths. I suspect it worked just fine.

its literary connections, but there is a good display of ceramics by the Culbone Potter, Waistel Cooper. Curiosities include a patten, a medieval shoe designed to keep the wearer's foot out of the mud, which was found in a chimney – where it will have been placed to ward off witchcraft. The Manor also has a small physic garden. Admission is free, but its trustees rely entirely on donations.

23 GREENCOMBE GARDENS

West Porlock TA24 8NU ℘ 01643 862363 ⌂ greencombe.org ☺ Apr–Jul 14.00–18.00 daily

Although open to the public, this is about as close to a secret garden as you can get. Mossy paths wind through flowering shrubs and dark trees, with surprises around every corner. And you're likely to be alone here, although Greencombe has the country's best collection of erythroniums (in the lily family), as well as other unusual plants.

Greencombe was the life's work of Joan Loraine, who died in 2016. All we see in the garden today is there because of her vision and dedication. It is now managed with the same enthusiasm by her nephew Rob Schmidt and his wife Kim.

Hidden off the road between Porlock and West Porlock, Greencombe is set on a hillside with an uninterrupted view of the sea. While the hillside shelters the garden in winter, it also hides the sun for two months of the year. When it returns in late January, Joan used to celebrate with a glass of sherry; the tradition has been continued by Rob and Kim.

"A simple wooden shelter protects the most beautiful woodcarving – of a mother and child."

The garden's steep slope is used to maximise our enjoyment of the planting. Overhead are oaks, conifers, sweet chestnuts and hollies – one holly is said to be the largest and oldest in the country. Among the ferns below are camellias and azaleas, roses and clematis, hydrangeas and rhododendrons. The hillside is quite dry, Porlock being sheltered from westerly winds by Exmoor's hills, so more than 25 tons of home-produced compost and leaf-mould are needed each year to keep the soil in good condition. Ruthless pruning is needed all year to stop the garden becoming a jungle.

Before you leave, don't miss the chapel at the far end of the garden. A simple wooden shelter protects the most beautiful woodcarving – almost life size – of a mother and child. This, and the peaceful garden, make Greencombe a very special place.

PORLOCK BAY OYSTERS

It's best not to be too anthropomorphic about oysters. If, like me, you get tearful reading *The Walrus and the Carpenter*, then the tribulations faced by these creatures on their way to our table won't help. The thing is, what oysters really like to do is sit around in sewage-rich sea, gently taking in all those delicious nutrients and postponing reproduction since it involves the hassle of changing sex. What oyster producers like to do is stress the oysters, which should really be doing their bit towards repopulating the seabed. This is done by varying the temperature of the water, which makes them think 'I'm going to die! I'd better have babies!' – and so they spawn, and the oyster producers have lots of tiny ones to nurture to maturity before bringing to our table.

Right, no more anthropomorphism. A local eight-year-old, after a visit to Porlock Weir, was more succinct when he wrote about the oyster experience: 'Oysters are grey and slimy and look like snot. But for some people to eat them is a delite but for others it would be a terrible punishment.' The delight aspect is what makes oyster farming worthwhile (the shellfish retail for £2–3 each) and why Porlock is making such a success of it.

It's an inspiring project. Porlock Weir, the home of Porlock Bay Oysters, was dredged for oysters in the mid 19th century, with medieval fish ponds used as holding pools and the then-new railway at Minehead transporting them speedily to London. Overfishing (from outside raiders) put paid to the trade until 2012 when the Parish Council, concerned at the lack of jobs in Porlock, set up Porlock Futures to come

up with some ideas. The consensus was oyster farming. History was on its side, the extreme tides were a help, and Porlock Weir had the cleanest water in the West Country (bad news for those sewage-loving oysters). So, how to fund it? Oysters take three years to grow to table-ready maturity so that financial gap had to be bridged. A not-for-profit Community Interest Company was set up and some money raised from grants, but the real breakthrough came through the generosity and enthusiasm of local people. The organisers wrote to 800 households asking for a loan of up to £1,000, interest-free if they wished. £157,000 was raised in that way and Porlock Bay Oysters became a reality.

Visiting the little depuration shed in Porlock Weir you'd never guess what a complicated business this is. Roger Hall explained to me that a specialist seed company in Guernsey provides the baby oysters, which are then transferred to a nursery site in Bantham on the River Avon where the water is warmer and less clean so that they thrive. When they reach restaurant size they come to Porlock to be 'finished' in the clean water for two months – the medieval fish traps once again serving as oyster beds – before spending their last few days in special tanks where UV light kills off all bacteria, a process called depuration.

You will find Porlock Bay Oysters (porlockbayoysters.co.uk) all over the West Country and you won't do better in quality. They have achieved top A-grade rating, making them a connoisseur's oyster. As you savour them, think of those 800 generous citizens of Porlock who made it all possible.

BEACHES, PEBBLES & MARSHES

Gill & Alistair Campbell

To the north of Porlock lies its extraordinary tidal saltmarsh. Walk down any lane towards the sea or drive to Porlock Weir and you will discover a marsh that is less than 20 years old.

The Bristol Channel has some of the highest tides in the world and the tidal saltmarsh sits below the mean high-water level. Twice a day, water rushes through a huge breach in the 2½-mile shingle bank, flooding the marsh with salt water. Only plants that are especially suited to this strange environment survive. There are large areas of common glasswort and sea blite, and many rare plants, too, like the everlasting pea, the lovely yellow horned poppy and Babbington's leek.

Until October 1996, this area was hardly affected by salt water; prize-winning barley was grown, there was good grazing and a freshwater lake. But a huge storm, part of Hurricane Lili, changed all that. The storm waters broke through the shingle ridge and salt water flooded the land. The National Trust and other landowners decided that it was time to let nature take its course and the flora and fauna are still adapting. Dotted everywhere here are the bleached skeletal remains of old, dead trees.

The storm also moved the remaining ridge inland by as much as 90 yards. Before the storm, the South West Coast Path crossed

24 PORLOCK WEIR

Cosily set under the hills [Porlock Weir is] altogether a spot made for peace and sweet do-nothing.

Penguin Guide to Somerset, 1939

The sea left Porlock's working harbour high and dry back in the Middle Ages, but at neighbouring Porlock Weir the shingle bar protected a tidal inlet and kept the harbour open – as it has been now for at least 1,000 years. In the 18th and 19th centuries, Porlock Weir was a busy little port, for coasters carrying timber across to South Wales and returning with coal. There was also an oyster fleet, and these delicacies are once again being farmed here (see box, page 83). Today yachts come and go from its sheltered marina and fishing boats bring in their catch. The row of thatched cottages next to the harbour provides a strand of brightness between the grey expanse of shingle and the dark woods above. The village has a large car park for walkers, with toilets and a small **natural history centre** (⊙ summer 13.30–17.00 Wed & Thu) at one end. Facing the harbour is a variety of places to eat, including the **Harbour**

the bay along the ridge. Today, that footpath would be well out at sea!

When the ridge moved it exposed the remains of an ancient aurochs. These large animals were the precursor of modern cattle but died out around 1500BC. There is also a submerged forest near Porlock Weir, but it is hard to spot except at exceptionally low tides.

There is no memorial to Saxon king Harold, who landed here in 1052 and burned down Porlock before marching to London, but you may come across the memorial commemorating the deaths of 11 US airmen in 1942. Their B-24 *Liberator* had been on submarine patrol. Returning in heavy rain and poor visibility, it crashed on the marsh. Only one airman survived. A German bomber met a similar fate.

Indeed, on the marsh's many paths we constantly find remnants of its recent history. Everything is built from huge beach pebbles – lime kilns abandoned around 1860; an ill-fated golf club house abandoned in 1914; pill boxes built during World War II, never used; and a cow shed abandoned in 1996.

The best way to truly appreciate this extraordinary landscape is to walk the marked footpath from Porlock Weir to Porlock or Bossington along the edge of Porlock Marsh. The route is clearly shown on the Croydecycle map.

Gallery and Café, which combines homemade cakes, good coffee, ceramics and paintings; and **Ziangs** (page 89) for Asian street food. A little **maritime museum** displays old photos and relics, including details of the lifeboat *Louisa*'s heroic rescue in 1899 (see box, page 60); next door is **Exmoor Glass**, where you can browse a huge selection of stained-glass objects. **Exmoor Adventures** (page 17) offers kayaking, stand-up paddle boarding and other water activities.

¶¶ FOOD & DRINK

A local treat that you may or may not find in the town is **Porlock Pie** – a concoction of venison, oysters and Exmoor ale. The prototype was made by Barrie Tucker of Luttrells of Dunster, a Porlock man, but at the time of writing no-one has taken on the task of creating them for what must surely be an eager market. Perhaps readers will start the ball rolling?

Locanda on the Weir Porlock Weir ✆ 01643 863300 ♂ locandaontheweir.co.uk. An Italian-influenced restaurant with rooms opened in 2018.Continental flair is provided by chef-proprietor Pio Catemario Di Quadri, the son of an Italian duke who learned the value of using the finest ingredients in the kitchens of the family palazzo. See ad, page 142.

ASC PHOTOGRAPHY/S

OPEN SPACES

There are countless opportunities for walking and wildlife-watching amid heather-clad landscapes.

HELEN HOTSON/S

NIGEL STONE

CHRIS EVELEIGH

1 Heather in bloom on Porlock Common. 2 Young red deer stags; the one in the foreground is 'in velvet'. 3 Dunkery Beacon. 4 Feral goat on the Valley of Rocks. 5 Wimbleball Lake in eastern Exmoor. 6 Walkers on the South West Coast Path near Little Hangman.

Piggy in the Middle 2 High St, Porlock ℘ 01643 862647 ☉ 17.00–21.00 daily, but open less frequently in winter. Specialise in excellent fish and chips cooked to order, whether eat-in or take-away. Also gourmet pies, desserts and vegan options. Small and popular, so you're advised to book ahead at busy times.

The Ship Inn (*'Bottom Ship'*) Porlock Weir ℘ 01643 863288 ⌂ shipinnporlockweir.co.uk. An attractive long, low, thatched building, with plenty of indoor and outdoor seating and traditional pub food. Popular with walkers and day visitors as well as locals, and bustles cheerfully on sunny days. It also has a tea room, with generous cream teas, home baking, and fresh coffee roasted by D J Miles & Co of Porlock (page 80).

TOP SHIP & BOTTOM SHIP

Janice Booth

The distinction is geographical rather than discriminatory: *Top Ship* is the local name for the Ship Inn in Porlock, while the Ship Inn down in Porlock Weir is known as *Bottom Ship*. Between the two of them, they've seen a fair amount of history. Bottom Ship, close to the harbour, is said to have whetted the whistle of the not-so-occasional smuggler in olden times, while Top Ship hosted a far more literary bunch.

The poet Robert Southey wrote a sonnet at Top Ship in 1798 (it starts 'Porlock, thy verdant vale so fair to sight'), and described to his brother a room where he spent the night: 'two long old dark tables with benches and an old chest composed its furniture, but there was an oval looking-glass, a decent pot de chambre and no fleas.' Samuel Taylor Coleridge was another of the Ship's literary customers; he and Southey both developed a taste for the local Porlock speciality, potted laver (seaweed), to the extent that Coleridge even asked a friend for more supplies of it after he'd left. R D Blackmore set some scenes of *Lorna Doone* in the inn, and H G Wells is also thought to have drunk there.

Built in 1290, Porlock's Ship is one of the oldest inns in England. Back in those days the sea came further inland than it does today and the inn was close to the shoreline – handy for smuggling, and no doubt the occasional intoxicating barrel found its way from surf to cellar. When stagecoaches were the means of transport up wearyingly steep Porlock Hill, spare horses were stabled at the inn to provide extra horsepower when needed.

As all good historic inns should, it does have a ghost, but she's a benevolent old lady of unknown origin and doesn't appear often. Less benevolently, it's thought that the infamous press gangs of the 18th century may have drunk there in order to 'persuade' some of the young men of Porlock, when they'd downed a flagon or so too many, to sign up for the navy.

After seven centuries the inn is still very much a part of Porlock life, hosting local functions and welcoming locals and visitors alike. And perhaps, if you indulge in the odd glass there, some ancient literary ghost may be sitting at your side …

The Ship Inn (*'Top Ship'*) High St, Porlock TA24 8QD ☎ 01643 862507 🖰 shipinnporlock. co.uk. A lovely whitewashed and thatched pub, serving both traditional pub food and more classic restaurant choices. The history is fascinating (see box, opposite).

Ziangs Porlock Weir ⊙ noon–17.00. With just two tables inside and a few outside, this unpretentious little place serves delicious Asian street food.

HORNER WOODS, STOKE PERO & DUNKERY BEACON

Of all the places in this section, I think these three – which can be linked in one long, strenuous walk – epitomise the pleasures of walking on (inland) Exmoor most satisfyingly. The National Nature Reserve of **Horner Woods** covers 1,000 or so acres and is one of Britain's largest remaining ancient oak forests. Along with the gnarled oaks are 330 species of lichen and mosses, giving the place a fairy-tale feel. The stream, Horner Water, adds to the attraction and provides a level walk – until you need to climb out of its deep valley. Like all places in the Holnicote Estate (page 97), the many paths are well signposted. **Stoke Pero Church** (page 90) gives a focal point to a walk, though be warned; the climb up the escarpment is very steep. Park at Horner and take the easy, level bridlepath that runs alongside the stream. After a little under two miles, Stoke Pero is signposted to the left where you gasp your way up the side of Ten Acre Cleeve to emerge by the little church. The return can be across cow pasture to Cloutsham Farm and back through bracken and heather to the woods. The Croydecycle *Horner & Dunkery* map shows these paths in great detail.

An easier three-mile walk from Webbers Post is described in a National Trust leaflet that can be picked up at the Clematis Gift Shop in Selworthy.

Above Horner Woods the moorland stretches in purple swathes towards **Dunkery Beacon**, at 1,703 feet the highest point in Exmoor. From August to mid-September, when the heather is in bloom, this is the most beautiful heathland. Few other places on Exmoor have so much heather, nor such a satisfactory contrast with the green, chequerboard fields in the valleys and the sea beyond. On a clear day you can see the mountains of Wales. For keen walkers there's the long ascent to Dunkery Beacon from Horner or Webbers Post, but most visitors avoid the hard slog by taking the almost level track that leads off from the lane that runs between Luccombe and Wheddon Cross. There's a small parking

area at Dunkery Gate (♀ SS89406, or roughly postode TA24 7AT) and
the walk to the Beacon will take only 15 minutes or so.

25 Stoke Pero Church

Stoke Pero is another superlative: Exmoor's highest church at 1,013
feet, and one of the three that were too remote to attract a parson,
according to the local ditty: 'Culbone, Oare and Stoke Pero, Parishes
three where no parson'll go.' Stoke Pero made do with a curate for
much of its history.

Not a lot remains of the original church; it was completely rebuilt by
Sir Thomas Acland in 1897, with the help of Zulu the donkey who
made the journey from Porlock twice a day carrying the timbers for the
roof. It's a most appealing and delightful little place, set companionably
next to some farm buildings. The interior is plain (though there's an
attractive barrel roof with carved floral-design bosses), candles are the
only lighting, and a little harmonium the only source of music. And
there's a framed drawing of Zulu the donkey on the wall.

26 TIVINGTON & WOOTTON COURTENAY

A turning to the right when heading for Minehead brings you to Wootton
Courtenay – which is not National Trust, has never seen a chocolate box
(except in the village shop), but is as traditional as they come.

The road, or rather lane, itself is full of interest, undulating past
woodland and groups of thatched cottages. One such is the unique
medieval chapel of ease at **Tivington**. It adjoins the house next door,
sharing a thatch, and once you've found the entrance you enter a tiny
room dominated by an open fireplace. There is little else inside the
simple interior save a couple of religious pictures and a tiny font, but
it oozes atmosphere and history. It's not easy to find; as the road rises
up, look for a thatched house next to a modern one on the right. The
signed entrance is at the side.

The much larger **All Saints' Church** in **Wootton Courtenay** dominates
the village with its unusual saddleback tower. The oldest part dates
from the mid 13th century and the church has an eccentric history. The
Norman owner of the manor gave it to a nearby French priory, which
was later dissolved by Henry VI who put the proceeds towards the
building of Eton College; as a consequence, the college reserved the
right to choose the church's rectors.

INCREDIBLE EDIBLES

Exmoor produces some of the best food you can find anywhere. The harsh, hilly environment lends itself to extensive livestock production. Cattle and sheep are allowed to graze over large areas and mature slowly, as nature intended. And on the more fertile soils a surprising variety of food and drink are produced. By eating food farmed in the region you are literally eating Exmoor – hence **Eat Exmoor** (⌂ visit-exmoor.co.uk/eat-exmoor), an award-winning 2018 initiative to bring together 'field to fork' people, from farmers to shops that sell local produce and restaurants that source their food and drink locally. These include blueberry growers (page 69), oyster farmers (see box, page 83) and even a marshmallow maker (see box, page 15). Arable farming is a challenge on Exmoor (see box, page 116), so organic farms such as Hindon (see box, page 100) are relatively rare because of the typically infertile soils and short growing season.

The following meat producers sell direct from the farm in meat boxes or individual packages, as well as through shops such as **Exmoor Food & Crafts** in Minehead (page 107).

Hidden Valley Pigs (see box, page 50)
Higher Hall Farm Brayford, west Exmoor ⌂ higherhallfarm.co.uk. Organic Red Ruby beef and Devon Closewool lamb.
Indicknowle Farm Nr Combe Martin. Red Ruby beef, lamb and pork, as well as home-produced cider.
Little Oak Farm Timberscombe, east Exmoor ⌂ littleoakfarm.co.uk. Pork from Middle White pigs (see box, page 115).
West Ilkerton Farm (see box, page 50)

A comprehensive website for Exmoor's food producers is ⌂ edibleexmoor.co.uk.

The region also has its food festivals, the main one being **Exmoor Food Festival** (⌂ exmoorfoodfest.com) held each February, when you can find special food deals throughout the area. Lynton and Lynmouth also have their **Lyn Food Festival** every September (⌂ lynfoodfest.co.uk), with lots of local stands.

Wootton Courtenay makes a good base for walking, with a choice of footpaths and Dunkery Beacon (page 89) less than four miles away – though relentlessly uphill.

The rather luxurious **Dunkery Beacon Country House Hotel** (⌂ dunkerybeaconaccommodation.co.uk) has an excellent restaurant open to non-residents, and a telescope for dark sky viewing.

THE WEST SOMERSET COAST: PORLOCK WEIR TO COUNTY GATE

The unpopulated stretch of the South West Coast Path between Porlock Weir and Lynmouth is popular with walkers but the whole stretch is 12 miles, so too long for many people. However, although a strong pair of legs is still necessary for its highlights, Culbone Church and Glenthorne Beach, shorter circular walks, make for a less strenuous day.

27 CULBONE CHURCH

The little church of St Beuno is utterly enchanting: the smallest working parish church in the country and surely one of the most remote. Although the vicar and some parishioners can bounce and

ADA, COUNTESS OF LOVELACE – & COMPUTER BUFF

Janice Booth

> I do not believe that my father was (or ever could have been) such a Poet as I shall be an Analyst...
>
> Ada Lovelace

Augusta Ada Byron was born in 1815, the only legitimate daughter of Lord Byron. Her mother Annabella's short and stormy marriage to the 'mad, bad' poet lasted only a year; they separated soon after Ada's birth and she never saw him again. Fearing that her daughter might inherit his unreliable temperament, Annabella had the little girl educated intensively in mathematics in order to discipline her mind. Ada did indeed become a formidable mathematician, but also a talented musician and linguist; she loved the arts, and as a young woman moved easily in London society. At a dinner party in 1833 she met the mathematician and inventor Charles Babbage and was fascinated by his mathematical 'engines', one of which was the forerunner of today's computers, while he was impressed by the speed with which this charming young socialite grasped exceptionally complex ideas.

In 1835 Ada married William King, becoming Countess of Lovelace when he was created Earl three years later. Their first home was the beautiful Ashley Combe at Porlock Weir, which William developed as a romantic Italianate country mansion to please his young bride. On Sundays they worshipped at tiny Culbone Church, grandly ensconced in the VIPs' box pew.

Ada still followed Babbage's work closely. In 1840 he spoke about his 'engines' at Turin

slither to it by Land Rover, for visitors the only access is on foot via the coastal path, a 2½-mile walk uphill from Porlock Weir. It's a lovely tramp through oak and beech forests with glimpses of the sea and welcome benches. *"Coleridge stayed nearby,* These woods were one of the favourite *where he had his opium-* haunts of Samuel Taylor Coleridge, who *induced vision of a* revelled in the local wildlife and views *'stately pleasure dome'."* of Wales across the water. He stayed in a farmhouse nearby where he had his opium-induced vision of a 'stately pleasure dome', which became the unfinished poem *Kubla Khan*, interrupted by the arrival of a person from Porlock.

Shortly after leaving the hamlet of Worthy and its thatched toll house, the path passes through two tunnels – intriguing since their original

University; the Italian transcript of the talks was translated into French, which Ada in turn translated into English – adding her own comprehensive notes, and outlining the fundamentals of computer programming and the main elements that any computer language required. She has been called the world's first female computer programmer, while Babbage more lyrically described her as an 'enchantress of numbers' and his 'fairy lady'. 'Fairy' she may have been, but also formidable: she is quoted as saying that being right entitled one to be rude, and reproved Babbage firmly when he altered something she had written.

Ada's talent was so far ahead of its time that intellectually she cut a solitary figure. When she died prematurely in 1852 after an eight-year struggle with cancer, her work faded largely from public memory, only resurfacing in 1953 when her notes on Babbage's analytical engine were republished.

Greater recognition followed. In 1979, the US Defense Department named an early, secret software program 'ADA' after her, and her image has appeared on Microsoft authenticity stickers. Tilda Swinton played her in the 1997 film *Conceiving Ada*; Ada Lovelace Day held annually in October aims to raise the profile of women in science, technology, engineering and maths; and 2015 saw publication of the partly fantasised graphic novel *The Thrilling Adventures of Lovelace and Babbage* by Sidney Padua. Last but by no means least, Porlock now celebrates Ada Lovelace Day with influential women speakers, and the town's computer centre is named after her – which surely the young 19th-century socialite could never remotely have envisaged.

County Gate to Glenthorne Beach

❋ Croydecycle *Lynton, Lynmouth & Doone* Valley; start: County Gate car park
♥ SS793486; just under 3 miles; quite strenuous – lots of ups & downs

This walk has been provided by Gill & Alistair Campbell, based on their book Porlock Walks.

From the car park cross the main road and turn left for about 100 yards – into Devon – then take the footpath on your right, signed Sister's Fountain and Coast Path. Where the track splits, go straight ahead through the wooden gate signed Coast Path. There are great views ahead across the combe and the Bristol Channel to Wales.

Continue downhill through a second gate at Seven Thorns where you turn right following the sign to Glenthorne Beach and the coast path. On your left below you is **Sister's Fountain**, a stone cross commemorating the place where, so the legend goes, St Joseph of Arimathea struck his staff into the ground to create a spring to slake his thirst on the way to Glastonbury.

Keep straight ahead, following signs to Culbone, walking downhill; at the next junction, Cosgate, turn left off the coast path, signed Glenthorne Beach, and after 100 yards or so turn sharp right at the footpath sign. Continue down the combe to a second right turn and cross a small stream – back into Somerset. The path, known as Ben's Path, undulates, keeping the fields and buildings of Glenthorne Home Farm on your left.

Beyond the farm, somewhat hidden in the trees, is **Glenthorne House**, now home to Sir Christopher Ondaatje, the writer and philanthropist. When you meet another track turn left and then, almost immediately, right, signed **Glenthorne Beach**; and then take a track left, heading downhill next to the stream, to reach the beach.

This is a real smugglers' beach. The goods were stored at County Gate which, being on the border of Devon and Somerset, was never searched. Out to sea you may spot gannets diving

purpose is difficult to fathom. In fact they were constructed when Ada, Countess of Lovelace, was living in the now-ruined Ashley Combe (see box, page 92). The tunnels routed tradesmen to the back entrance of the house, so she was spared the unpleasantness of meeting any of the lower orders as she made her way to her bathing hut.

After about an hour of walking, quite suddenly you round a bend and the little grey church appears below you, squatting in a clearing with its spire, set slightly askew, reaching hopefully towards the treetops. Legend has it that this is actually the top of the Porlock Church spire

for shoals of fish. When this happens, keep an eye out for the black fins of porpoises.

Leave the beach by retracing your steps up the same track, turning right at the first track junction and then left at the second. Where Ben's Path leaves to your right, carry straight on, uphill, signed Yenworthy Combe. Continue climbing, keeping the stream on your left.

Glenthorne Pinetum was planted by the Reverend Walter Halliday between 1840 and 1870 and contains many exotic trees, including dawn redwood, Chinese cow's tail pine and western hemlock. It was the first time many of these trees had been planted in England. One *Wellingtonia* giant redwood is among the tallest in the country, at over 150 feet. On the left are the remains of an ice house and of trout breeding ponds. Further up the slope there is an information board, on the right of the path.

When you reach the coast path track, turn right on to it so that you can return to County Gate and your car.

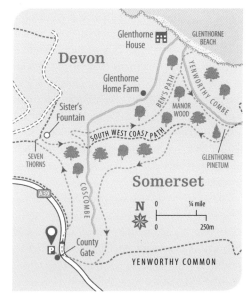

that blew off in a gale and landed here. Or maybe was snapped off by a giant and placed here. An examination of the graveyard is rewarding, with the local family Red being well represented. Look out for the stone of Ethel Red; presumably always unready.

The name Culbone is a corruption of Kil Beun, or church of St Beuno (pronounced Bayno), a Welsh missionary saint. The interior seats 33 at a pinch. There's no room for anything except the pews, including a box pew for the Lovelace family, a tiny harmonium squeezed into a corner, spattered with candle wax, and the Norman font, so roughly carved that the marks of the stonemason's chisel are still visible. There has probably been a church here since Saxon times, and bits have been added through the centuries. One of the oldest features is the twin window on the north side of the chancel, which may be a thousand years old, with a strange face carved above it that looks more like a cat than a man. Beyond it is a window where the decorative tracery that holds in the glass is made from wood, not stone. And between the two is a 'leper squint' – a tiny window at eye level that supposedly allowed the lepers who had been banished to the surrounding woodland to get a glimpse of a church service.

It would be hard not to be moved by this little church. In the booklet telling its story the author writes: 'Its walls are saturated with centuries of worship and it is tended with a care that reveals the devotion of its congregation.' Indeed.

To return to Porlock Weir you can either retrace your steps or continue following the coastal path, along and then up the same track that the vicar uses to access the church in the ecclesiastical 4x4, to Silcombe Farm (this is a steep climb), then head east along quiet lanes until you reach the toll road. A footpath runs parallel to this road, alongside Worthy Combe through the lovely twisted oaks of Worthy Wood or, if you have energy to spare, take the bridle path deeper into the woods, to emerge east of Porlock Weir.

EAST OF PORLOCK:
THE NATIONAL TRUST VILLAGES

At the edge of Exmoor is the lozenge of glorious countryside between Porlock, Minehead, the A39 and the sea. It has the coastal path running over Selworthy Beacon, and an infinite choice of woodland trails and quiet lanes taking you through arguably the prettiest villages of Exmoor: Luccombe, Allerford, Bossington and Selworthy. These four National Trust villages are quintessentially rural England with their thatched cottages strung along narrow lanes. Look out for the lateral chimneys, set in the side of the cottage rather than the end, and often incorporating a bulging bread oven. And talking of baking, it feels like there must be a higher concentration of tea rooms in this area than any other place in England. Footpaths and quiet lanes connect all the villages so it's easy and rewarding to devise a walk that includes them all. The Croydecycle *Porlock* map will give you plenty of ideas and the National Trust car parks have information boards that describe walks and show clear maps.

The villages are part of the Holnicote Estate, comprising around 12,000 acres of eastern Exmoor, which were inherited by the Acland family in 1745 and owned by them until donated to the National Trust in 1944 by Sir Richard Dyke Acland, the 15th baronet. It includes four miles of coast, a chunk of the moor including Dunkery and Selworthy beacons, the great Horner Woods – one of the largest National Nature Reserves in Britain – and the villages of Selworthy, Allerford, Bossington, Horner and Luccombe. There are more than 170 cottages and 144 farms on the estate.

The family seem to have been benevolent landowners and the Acland touch is everywhere, from the charming Lynch Chapel of Ease between Allerford and Bossington, which was used as a barn until restored by Sir Thomas Acland, to the memorial shelter above Selworthy Woods, inscribed with lines of poetry.

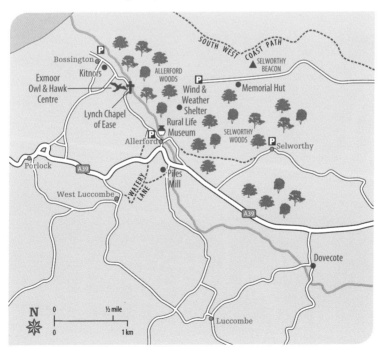

LOCAL LIFE

Whether in a town or village, rural life carries on at its own pace.

1 The ford and packhorse bridge at Malmsmead. **2** Hunting the Earl of Rone in Combe Martin. **3** Bossington, one of the villages in the Holnicote Estate managed by the National Trust. **4** Porlock's High Street. **5** Exmoor is not only moorland: the view towards Winsford.

HELEN HOTSON/S

@EXMOORNATIONALPARKAUTHORITY

DAVIDYOUNG/S

CHRISTIAN MUELLER/S

A MORAL DUTY

Roger and Penny Webber have farmed organically for nearly 20 years, a shift from generations of conventional farming in this corner of Exmoor. We chatted over my breakfast of Roger's delicious hand-made pork sausages, and eggs from the hens that were scratching around the yard.

'Why did we go organic? It really came about during difficult times in the 1990s – farming is always a challenge, and we had had bad experiences with the inferior ingredients in animal feeds and we hated putting toxins on our precious land. So we decided to try this alternative way to farm. A slower, less intensive way. At that time there was financial support for changing to organic farming which was a great help. It took a while, but gradually we started seeing improvements with the health of our animals and the land. I saw wild flowers, insects and other creatures I'd never seen there before such as lizards, butterflies, ladybirds and the like.'

Roger was born at Hindon Farm. His grandfather was a tenant farmer for Sir Richard Acland, the original landowner, then Roger's father took on the tenancy and, years later, passed it on to Roger and Penny – along with a lot of debt. The next generation will take over eventually: 'Our daughter Emily and her partner Chris are farm partners. For all of us farming is a way of life and worth the hard work – as is running the B&B. But sharing our farm with our guests is very rewarding. Our first couple still return after 30 years! We are proud to be organic farmers.'

Hindon Organic Farm has won many awards including National Organic Producers of the Year, the Sustainability Award from South West Tourism and Food Heroes' Beautiful Farm Award, but it is a more subtle reward that brings the most pleasure. 'We have a moral duty to our animals,' Roger said, summing up the ethos that makes the long days worthwhile.

28 LUCCOMBE & HORNER

The essence of unspoiled Exmoor, **Luccombe** (not to be confused with the scatter of houses that is West Luccombe) is just far enough off the beaten path to thin the influx of visitors. 'They all go to Selworthy – thank God,' said one resident when we complimented him on his village. The church of St Mary is lovely inside and out. Lift the rug at the altar end of the nave, and admire the 17th-century brass of William Harrison, resplendent in his ruff and gown. Next to the church is a thatched cottage that surely must once have been a long house, with cattle living at one end.

Before you get to the village, soon after you leave the A39, you'll come to **Blackford House** (the road makes a right-angled turn here). A medieval dovecote, circular in shape and owned by the National

Trust, makes an interesting visit. It's a curious building, over 20 feet high, with a small door to let you inside. The domed roof has an opening, an oculus, which allowed the birds to fly in and out. Around the walls are 11 rows of nesting holes, more than 300 of them. The dovecote was probably built in Norman times. Wealthy Normans kept domesticated pigeons to provide a luxury food, the tender meat of the young pigeons or squabs. It was illegal for anyone except lords of the manors and parish priests to keep pigeons until the 1800s. A breeding pair produced ten to 12 young birds a year. The keeper would check the dovecote frequently and remove any squabs that were near fledging – about a month old. These birds were nearly as large as adult birds but, as their flight muscles had never been used, their meat was exceptionally tender.

The dovecote can be visited at any time, free of charge.

A mile northwest of Luccombe is the hamlet of **Horner**, comprising a few cottages and two tea rooms, both equally seductive if you feel the urge for a cream tea. It's the starting point for some walks in the adjacent Horner Woods (page 89).

29 ALLERFORD

This village is crammed with interest: a 17th-century packhorse bridge and the delightful **Rural Life Museum and Victorian Schoolroom** (🖉 01643 862529 ☉ Apr–Oct 10.00–16.00 Tue–Fri, 13.30–16.30 Sat & Sun) housed in the old village school. The original desks, benches and slates are still there, and there is some Victorian children's clothing for modern-day kids to try on. The museum houses a large assortment of artefacts that would have been used by our rural ancestors. There is a handy car park for walkers.

Nearby is the **Exmoor Owl & Hawk Centre** (West Lynch Farm, TA24 8HJ 🖉 01643 862816 ♂ exmoorfalconry.co.uk). Owls are the main attraction here – many different species, including a majestic grey owl – as well as the more familiar hawks. There is also a palmnut vulture. In addition to the flying displays, and an in-depth bird-of-prey experience, the centre offers **riding** with a difference. The horses go 'barefoot and bitless' (see box, page 12).

The centre also serves lunches and teas, and B&B is available.

Just off the A39 is **Piles Mill**, a working mill (open to the public) and study centre that also holds regular activities for children.

"The sheer delight of this heathery national park, where moor meets sea, means that visitors can't help but take their time."

HELEN HOTSON/S

FAMILY PICNIC PLACES ON EXMOOR

Gill & Alistair Campbell

Whether you are looking for a bench with a view or a grassy meadow with a stream, you can find it on Exmoor. And everyone you talk to has their own favourite. Here are a few that local people have recommended, listed from west to east.

Watersmeet ♥ SS744487. Park in the linear car park on the A39 and walk down to the river or leave your car in Lynmouth and walk up river. There are grassy banks, the odd bench, lots of water to splash about in and a National Trust tea shop, in case you forgot the picnic!
Countisbury ♥ SS750502. Park in the car park by the Blue Ball pub on the A39 and walk seawards past the church. Here there is a long grassy bank and a 180° view. Pick a calm day.
Robber's Bridge ♥ SS820464. A little way south of the A39 and east of Oare, again with a lovely river and views down the Doone Valley.
Allercombe Meadow ♥ SS894430. Set off the road between Webbers Post and Cloutsham, this sheltered meadow is ideal for picnics. There is room enough for a game of French cricket and a lovely stream to dip in, to paddle in, or to dam.

30 BOSSINGTON

Handy for some relaxation after doing the shore walk from Porlock, this picturesque little village has particularly good examples on many of the cottages of the local lateral chimneys with bread ovens. On a fine day the tables on the lawn of **Kitnors Tea Room** provide a leafy haven of sunshine and birdsong. There are tables inside for wet days, too. The thatched house dates from the 15th century and the teas are really special, with an excellent selection of cakes.

31 SELWORTHY

This village is probably the best starting point for a walk around the region, giving you a choice of high moorland walking, or valley and village, or a combination of both. It's another chocolate-box village with a spacious green and many thatched cottages. The church here is a startling sight when one is accustomed to the usual grey towers that are so typical of England. This is whitewashed – or rather lime-washed – as were most other churches in the region though few are maintained so conscientiously. Before exploring inside, take a look at the view through the open door: beautiful! The interior is full of interest, with a fine wagon roof, the beams ending in wooden angels, and carved bosses. An

Webbers Post ♥ SS902439. South of Horner and Luccombe, Webbers Post has easy parking, benches and a huge view over the Holnicote Estate. Walk a little way north from the parking to find the Wind and Weather Hut, handy for shelter on a windy day. This is a good place for flying kites.

Horner ♥ SS897454. This small village southeast of Porlock has a good car park with toilets and picnic benches. The village green is a favourite picnic spot with a shallow stream, ideal for playing in. For the more adventurous, head into the ancient woods and find your own shady glade.

Bossington ♥ SS897480. This beautiful village east of Porlock has picnic sites by the car park – benches, toilets and even two barbecues. There is a river to play in. It is an easy stroll to the pebble beach or up on to Hurlstone Point – more benches and stunning views.

Bury Castle ♥ SS917471. Slowly climb from Selworthy or walk across from the North Hill road. There is little left of Bury Castle but you can picnic among its grassy banks and enjoy spacious views. A great place for hide and seek!

hourglass by the pulpit ensured the sermons ended on time. Over the font is a rather predatory-looking wooden dove incorporated into the mechanism for raising and lowering the lid. And there's an absolutely wonderful chest, all worm-eaten wood and ancient iron, straight out of *Treasure Island*. It's thought to be over 400 years old and is now used for contributions to the church's upkeep.

Light lunches and cream teas are served in the garden of nearby **Periwinkle Cottage**, possibly the most photographed tea room in the West. The selection of cakes is terrific, as is the variety of ploughman's lunches. Above it is the **Clematis Gift Shop** which, in addition to souvenirs, has leaflets describing various walks in Selworthy and Horner Wood.

"Nearby Periwinkle Cottage is possibly the most photographed tea room in the West."

From Selworthy you can walk uphill through these woods to the South West Coast Path. All paths are well signposted, and the woods are a rewarding mix of mature oak and birch. Near the road at the top you'll come across a 'wind and weather shelter' dedicated to Sir Thomas Dyke Acland who died in 1871. Poems by Heber and Keble are engraved on each end.

MINEHEAD & EASTERN EXMOOR

The [carriage] drive from Minehead to Porlock is one of the most beautiful in Somersetshire. On each side of the road rise hills of varied outline, covered with fern and heather, whilst the rugged valley charms by its abundant woods, grouped over broken ground and mingled with cornfields.

A Handbook for Travellers in Somerset, 1899

Minehead, though outside the national park, is its eastern gateway and proudly the beginning of the 630-mile South West Coast Path. Within this part of the park is its most appealing town, Dunster, home to one of the most interesting castles in the county, owned for 18 generations by the Luttrell family whose name permeates the region. To the south is Wheddon Cross, which most drivers approaching Exmoor from Tiverton will pass through and which comes into its own during its Snowdrop Festival. Dulverton, on the southern edge of the moor, is the national park headquarters. Travel east from here to Wimbleball Lake where you can experience active Exmoor in all its watery forms. And, by the way, the area of the national park to the east of the A396 is known as the Brendon Hills, not to be confused with Brendon Common near Oare.

32 MINEHEAD

Tourist information: The Beach Hotel, The Avenue, Minehead TA24 5AY ✆ 01643 702624 ⌂ mineheadbay.co.uk ⊘ summer 10.00–16.00 Tue–Sat, 11.00–16.00 Sun, winter 10.30–15.00 Sat & Sun

Whether Butlins or the start of the South West Coast Path, amusement arcades or a network of leafy foot and cycle paths high above the town, Minehead has something for everyone; but the Slow traveller will be drawn to the western and upper parts of the town where history and rural pursuits take precedence.

Minehead is the start/finish point of the West Somerset Railway and the TIC is located near the station; it can provide you with plenty of inspiration to keep you busy for a few hours.

Most shops and restaurants are on The Avenue, while the posh hotels and B&Bs are up the steep hills that lead to Higher Town, with their elegant large houses and tumbling gardens. Among the shops that draw locals to Minehead is the excellent **Toucan Wholefoods** (3 The Parade) with its vegetarian restaurant upstairs. Continuing the food

MINEHEAD'S HOBBY HORSE

Whereas Padstow's hobby horse gets national media coverage, Minehead's, which is just as old and weird, is known only to locals. And if you're thinking you know what a hobby horse looks like because your kids have one, not Minehead's you don't! Read on ...

Like Padstow's, the origin of this festival is lost in the mists of time, but it's certainly been going on for a long time. The earliest recorded mention of the event in Minehead is in 1792 but it's likely to have started centuries before that.

The hobby horse comes out of hiding on the evening of 30 April at the Old Ship Aground, and starts its parade at dawn on 1 May when it twirls, sways and gambols around the area, including a trip to Dunster Castle, accompanied by men playing drums and an accordion. This goes on for three days. Very little of the hobby horse resembles a horse – it's much more like a boat, reinforced by the fact that 'Sailors Horse' is painted on its sides, amid decorative rings. It has a tail, however, with which it chastises onlookers who fail to make a donation (which goes to charity).

On the last day it might be confronted by the 'Town Horse', with a fight ensuing.

All in all it's a weird and wonderful spectacle, rivalling Combe Martin's Earl of Rone (see box, page 30).

---

theme, Minehead has one of the longest-running **farmers' markets** in the area; it's held every Friday from March to December. Lovers of fresh produce should head to **Exmoor Food & Crafts** (4 The Avenue), a co-operative of food producers and craftspeople. Porlock's Churchgate Gallery (page 80) has a sister in Minehead, the **Courtyard Gallery** on Friday Street, with similar upmarket exhibitions.

Walkers will drift along to the western part of the seafront since, even if you're only planning to walk the seven or so miles into Porlock, it's more or less mandatory to have your photo taken next to the sculpture that marks the start of the 630-mile South West Coast Path. It depicts a pair of hands holding an Ordnance Survey map.

If you are in Minehead for the May bank holiday you're in for a treat: the **Hobby Horse Festival** is one of only two in the country (see box, above).

FOOD & DRINK

Alcombe Fish Bar Brook St, Minehead ☎ 01643 703220 ⏱ 11.30–13.45 & 17.00–21.00 Tue–Sat. Tucked away in a side street, this is considered by locals to serve the best fish and chips in the town: 'sit on the prom to eat them or drive up to North Hill.'

Cream 20A The Avenue, Minehead ☎ 01643 708022 ⋕ cafecream.co.uk ⏱ 09.00–20.00

daily, until 21.00 in summer. A crisp, modern – and licensed – place serving excellent breakfasts, light lunches and, in the summer, dinners, with good coffee and cakes at any time. Popular with locals.

Old Ship Aground Harbourside, Quay St, Minehead ✆ 01643 703516 🖉 theoldshipaground.com. A beautiful traditional pub in a lovely location on the harbour, close to the start of the South West Coast Path. Open fires in the winter, outdoor seating in the summer, and excellent food.

Passioni Italiane 3a Holloway St, Minehead ✆ 01643 818130 ⊙ 07.30–15.00 Mon–Sat. A very popular and highly praised Italian restaurant open for breakfast and lunch. Owners Gavin and Christina go the extra mile.

The *Quantock Belle* This is food on the move! The West Somerset Railway periodically runs a special dining train that oozes nostalgia for anyone who remembers the 'Good Old Days' when meals on wheels meant being called for the first sitting. It is extremely popular so book well in advance (through the WSR website; page 16).

33 DUNSTER

Tourist information: Dunster National Park Centre, Dunster Steep TA24 6SE ✆ 01643 821835 ⊙ 10.00–17.00 daily

Dunster sits just within the national park, and is deservedly the most visited small town in eastern Exmoor. It's also one of the best-preserved medieval villages in England, with car-harassing narrow streets and the backdrop of a splendid castle and the folly-topped mound of Conygar Wood. Until 2011 the pavements comprised ancient cobblestones that looked lovely but made for painful and sometimes dangerous walking. Parts have now been replaced by paving slabs, which are less charming but easier on the feet.

The shops are tasteful, selling high-quality goods; the traffic is controlled; and there are lots of quality pubs, tea shops and snack bars. Among the shops is the excellent **Deli**, which sells a good selection of local crafts and a huge range of local beers and ciders.

It's strange to think that in the 12th century Dunster Haven was a busy port. When the shore became land, the town switched its activities to the wool trade so successfully that the local cloth was known as 'Dunsters'. The octagonal Yarn Market was built in 1609 to protect the wool traders from the Exmoor weather; it serves a similar purpose for damp tourists today.

Medieval towns like this often feel claustrophobic, but Dunster revels in open spaces and enclosed public gardens. Across one such space,

"*Dunster is one of the best-preserved medieval villages in England, with car-harassing narrow streets and the backdrop of a splendid castle.*"

109

the Village Garden, is the dovecot, which probably dates from the 14th century and still has the nest holes. It originally belonged to the priory but after the Dissolution of the Monasteries was sold to the Luttrells (the family that lived at Dunster Castle for 18 generations). Young pigeon, squab, was a luxury food, and until the 17th century only lords of the manor and parish priests were allowed to keep pigeons.

"This is the perfect approach: peaceful and uncrowded with only the sound of birdsong and the river."

Near the dovecote is a lovely little church garden, and the red sandstone church of St George. First impressions are of a gloriously intricate wagon roof, some good bosses, and a font with a complicated cover. And the famous screen. Now, most old churches have screens, and many have screens as beautifully carved as this one, with fan vaulting to support the weight of the rood. But none, anywhere, has a screen this length, stretching across the full 54-foot width of the church (see box, opposite).

A rural lane running alongside a stream leads to the **Water Mill**. Dating from the 17th century and grinding wheat daily to produce flour for its shop and local bakeries, it's an interesting place to visit and the tea room serves very tasty light meals. Continue past the mill and you enter the spacious gardens of Dunster Castle. This is the perfect approach to the castle: peaceful and uncrowded with, when I was there, only the sound of birdsong and the river. A path winds round to the main, steep entrance to the castle, which is also easily accessed from both West and High streets. Be warned, though; it is a *very* steep climb (Angina Hill, they call it) from the town or the castle car park so it's not really suitable for visitors with health problems.

Dunster by Candlelight

In early December, this winter festival (∂ dunsterbycandlelight.co.uk) plunges the town into darkness save for lanterns. A procession, led by stilt-walkers, wends its way through the streets, which are banned to cars, and cafés and shops that are normally closed in the winter open for business. An unmissable experience.

The Castle

Dunster Castle is mentioned in the Domesday Book and was home to the Luttrell family from 1405 until it was handed over to the National

DIVINE SEPARATION: DUNSTER CHURCH SQUABBLE

Why does Dunster Church have the longest screen in England? The reason had nothing to do with the worship of God but everything to do with sour relations. The Benedictine monks from the priory had used the church since its founding in about 1090, while the townspeople, with their vicar, carried out the usual church duties of services, marriages, baptisms and burials in the same church. Then, in the 15th century, a dispute arose about who did what, where and when. Nasty tricks were played, such as tying up the bells out of the reach of the monks, and even imprisoning them for a time at the east end of the church.

Things got so heated that the matter went to arbitration at Glastonbury in 1498, and the verdict was that a screen should be built to separate the parishioners and their vicar from the monks. The nave belonged to the town and the chancel to the priory. This seems to have left everyone relatively happy – at least until the Dissolution of the Monasteries some 40 years later.

Trust in 1974. This unbroken span of ownership gives it a unique appeal, with features typical of each century of privileged, but usually charitable, living. It is, simply put, gorgeous. The ornate plasterwork on the ceilings, the alabaster fireplaces, and the intricately carved grand-scale wooden staircase are particularly impressive, but so are the paintings, and the furniture, and even the bath (installed in 1870 and one of the first cast-iron baths in England). Look too at the unique leather paintings in the Leather Room, with scenes from Shakespeare's *Antony and Cleopatra*. They were done in the Netherlands in 1681 and are not to modern taste, but the technique is fascinating.

Tours of the attics and kitchens give you added insight into how a large house like this was run in the late 19th century, through its time as a convalescent home for US soldiers in World War II to the innovations introduced for the last Luttrell to live here, Alys. It's very Downton Abbey.

As you explore, remember to look at the view over the Bristol Channel from any of the east-facing windows. You can clearly see the distinctive islands of Steepholm and Flatholm, and the Welsh coast.

When you have finished with the house, don't miss the Dream Garden created by, or for, Alys Luttrell. At any season it's a riot of flowers penned in by little box hedges, with paths winding between them and a backdrop of the church tower.

ANTHONY CHRISTIE

SLOW DAYS OUT

Take your time to enjoy the many sights and activities that Exmoor National Park has to offer.

@EXMOORNATIONALPARKAUTHORITY

@EXMOORNATIONALPARKAUTHORITY

VISIT EXMOOR

1 This little steam train sets out from Woody Bay Station. 2 Flying the birds at the Owl & Hawk Centre, Allerford. 3 Withypool tea room with its historic petrol pumps. 4 Greencombe Gardens, West Porlock. 5 Dunster Village Garden with its historic dovecote. 6 The cliff railway connecting Lynton to Lynmouth. 7 Planning a route with Discovery Safaris. 8 The Quantock Heritage Bus runs between Minehead and Lynmouth during the summer.

¶¶ FOOD & DRINK

Chapel House Tea Rooms 2 West St ✆ 01643 822343 ⊙ 09.30–16.00 Wed–Mon. Bang opposite the road to the castle, serving very good lunches and teas, including savoury scones and cream teas.

Cobblestones 24a High St ✆ 01643 821595 ⊘ cobblestonesdunster.co.uk ⊙ 10.30–16.00 Sun–Tue, 10.30–20.00 Wed–Sat. Meals include a lunchtime Sunday roast and cream teas in comfortable surroundings. And there's a sunny walled garden for the summer. Can get busy, therefore slow, in the holiday season.

Hathaways 6–8 West St ✆ 01643 821725 ⊘ hathawaysofdunster.com ⊙ 19.00–22.00 Mon, Tue & Thu–Sat. An upmarket Italian restaurant in a lovely old cottage. Booking essential.

Luttrell Arms Restaurant (Psalter's Restaurant) 32–36 High St ✆ 01643 821555 ⊘ luttrellarms.co.uk. An award-winning restaurant in this elegant, dog-friendly inn. All meals, including breakfast, are open to non-residents. It has a gorgeous garden for summer and open fires in winter.

Reeves Restaurant 20–22 High St ✆ 01643 821414 ⊘ reevesrestaurantdunster.co.uk ⊙ from 19.00 (last orders 21.00) Tue–Sat, noon–14.00 Sun. Indisputably the best restaurant in the area, drawing clientele from Porlock and beyond for an exceptional night out.

34 TIMBERSCOMBE

Just off the A396, about three miles southwest of Dunster, is this unpretentious village of red sandstone houses with an interesting church, St Petrock's, also built in red stone. One of its finest features is the ancient oak door from the 15th century; the hinges are even older, perhaps from the 13th century. Prominent in the porch is the gravestone of a schoolmaster, William Brownwood, who served under Nelson in the Battle of Trafalgar. An arch ends in two heads, one with a splendid dreadlocky beard, and inside there's another fierce-looking gentleman with a crinkly beard on one of the wagon roof's bosses. Look, too, at the beautifully carved, fan-vaulted screen, probably made in Dunster. On the south wall are the remains of a mural that I first took to be an angel, but is in fact David playing his harp (presumably to soothe King Saul, a popular Bible story).

Timberscombe is also the home of the enchanting Middle White pigs that live at Little Oak Farm (see box, opposite).

35 WHEDDON CROSS & SNOWDROP VALLEY

Wheddon Cross is the highest village in Exmoor, a friendly place that gained importance as a major crossroads – so, a natural travellers'

ME OBESE? HAPPY PIGS AT TIMBERSCOMBE

The Middle White pigs that enjoy rooting around in the fields of Little Oak Farm have squashed-in noses and prick ears. They are also a rare breed, listed as an endangered species, leading farmer Pam to tell me that 'there are more giant pandas than Middle Whites'. The original porker, and prized for its high-quality meat, the breed lost favour when the public demanded leaner pork after World War II. The Middle Whites do tend to have a good layer of fat, which enhances the flavour and texture of the pork and is now considered a virtue. Pam and her husband Andy sell their pork products at farmers' markets in Exmoor and to local hotels.

While most of the pigs are kept on a fairly strict diet, much to their indignation, the pigs in one group are so big their bellies almost touch the ground, and their little eyes peer out under folds of fat. 'They can eat as much as they want!' said Pam – and pigging out is a porcine speciality. It's all to do with lardo, prized by gourmet restaurants, and for which the Middle White is perfect. To put it crudely, this is the fat off a larger pig's back, and Little Oak Farm supplies it to a charcuterie producer in Dorset, who then sells the finished product to top hotels and restaurants throughout the UK. So these pigs live off the fat of the land, and give it back at the end of their lives.

For information on where and how to buy these meat products, visit their website at ⊘ littleoakfarm.co.uk.

rest. There's a well-used village hall, **Moorland Hall**, which hosts fundraising groups during the snowdrop season, when it becomes the Snowdrop Café, plus an excellent supermarket/petrol station. You can buy everything consumable here, including Porlock oysters.

The village comes into its own each February when North Hawkwell Wood is carpeted with snowdrops. **Snowdrop Valley** is owned by the Badgworthy Land Company and is an ESA (Environmentally Sensitive Area). It's a gentle 45-minute circular walk alongside the River Avill, which used to drive a sawmill; the remains of a weir can still be seen. During the snowdrop season the narrow road leading to the valley is closed to traffic so visitors must walk there along a choice of two woodland routes, or take the Park and Ride bus that runs from the Wheddon Cross car park (next to the Rest and Be Thankful Inn). A map of the walks is available from the ticket office. Since snowdrops bloom in February, the wettest month, be prepared for deep, glutinous mud. In 2018, the bus driver told us to look out for the 'increasingly fat' robin that has mastered the art of flirting with visitors. He duly appeared and got his reward.

FARMING ON EXMOOR

Victoria Eveleigh

Although Exmoor is a national park, three-quarters of it is privately owned, and approximately 80% of the land area is farmed. Even the ancient woodlands and open moorland have been shaped by centuries of human activity. The woodlands have been managed for charcoal and wood, as well as cover for game, while the moorland was largely created by deforestation and climate change during the Iron Age, about 2,500 years ago. If the moorland was not grazed regularly, most of it would return to scrub or woodland.

Farming traditionally provides food, fuel and fibre for people, and the farms on Exmoor have produced all three with varying degrees of success depending on the climate and economic conditions of the time. For instance, wool used to be an expensive commodity but it's hardly worth the cost of shearing sheep nowadays.

Exmoor's topography, poor soils, high rainfall and inaccessibility mean that the options for farmers are limited. Most of the land isn't suited to arable crops, especially with modern farming methods, so grassy fields bounded by stockproof hedges are a common sight and Exmoor farmers tend to specialise in sheep and beef cattle. Some still remain faithful to the local breeds – notably Exmoor Horn and Devon Closewool sheep, and Devon cattle – but all sorts of different breeds and cross-breeds are kept.

It is estimated that at the beginning of the 20th century about half of Exmoor was moorland, but by the end of the century the area had shrunk to 27%, much of this being

The area is anyway predisposed to snowdrops, and you'll see bursts of them beside the road as you drive to Wheddon Cross. Make a day of it and have a meal in the village.

¶¶ FOOD & DRINK

Exmoor House ✆ 01643 841432 ⌂ exmoorhouse.co. This B&B open its doors to non-residents during the snowdrop season for homemade soup, cream teas and a variety of delicious cakes.

The Rest and Be Thankful ✆ 01643 841222 ⌂ restandbethankful.co.uk. Ideal for a lunchtime warm-up after Snowdrop Valley, including a carvery on Sundays, or a substantial evening meal.

36 DULVERTON

Tourist information: Dulverton National Park Centre, 7–9 Fore St, TA22 9EX ✆ 01398 323841 ⊙ 10.00–17.00 daily

Dulverton seems to have everything going for it: lovely surroundings,

lost in the nine years between 1957 and 1966. This seems ironic, as Exmoor was designated a national park in 1954 in response to the threat posed to its landscape by plans for large-scale conifer plantations. As it turned out, an equally serious threat came from farming due to post-war government subsidies designed to encourage the production of affordable food, together with technological advances that made the reclamation of moorland relatively easy. Government grants to drain and improve land continued well into the 1970s, even though the loss of moorland was causing alarm.

Concern about the preservation of Exmoor's moorland led to local schemes from the 1980s onwards, as well as later nationwide incentives for farmers to manage their land in a way prescribed by the government.

Lots of rules and regulations govern what happens on modern farms, and farming is becoming an increasingly complex job. At the time of writing, the spectre of Brexit hangs over us. Nobody knows what will happen to British agriculture, but it's clear that the concept of natural capital will be central to any new support systems. Besides producing food, fibre and fuel farmers will be expected to deliver a wide range of environmental goods like flood mitigation, soil conservation, carbon storage, biodiversity, biosecurity and cultural ecosystem services. That's a lot to worry about!

A good way of learning more about farming on Exmoor is to stay on a farm during your visit or check out the many farmers' markets or farm shops in the region. For more information, see the box on page 91.

plenty to see and do, yet manages to avoid any suggeston of being a tourist hotspot. No wonder the national park chose to have its headquarters here.

Like so many places in Exmoor, Dulverton has its **Lorna Doone** association and there's a small statue of the young woman outside Exmoor House. It's actually of Lady Lorna Dugal 'who, in the seventeenth century, was kidnapped in childhood by the outlaw Doones of Badgworthy', so was probably the inspiration for the novel. The hero of the story, John Rudd (known as Jan when he was a boy) first sets eyes on Lorna as a little girl 'dark-haired and very wonderful, with a wealthy softness on her' as she sits in a handsome coach near Dulverton. Later, near Dunkery Beacon, he unknowingly sees her again, carried across the saddle of one of the Doone brigands, back to their hideout.

The town's attractions include a 17th-century bridge over the River Barle, a variety of independent shops, some good restaurants and the excellent Heritage Centre. Shops include the greengrocer H&M

River Barle circuit from Dulverton

❉ OS Explorer map OL9 or Croydecycle *Dulverton & Tarr Steps*; start: Bridge car park, TA22 9HJ; 3.8 miles; fairly easy (some steep inclines)

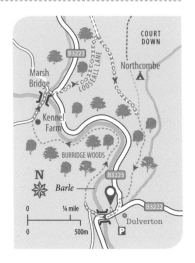

Cross the bridge and turn immediately right along a lane, which soon becomes a track leading uphill (do not take the road to the left). You are heading for Marsh Bridge along a footpath, signposted Tarr Steps, which curves around the end of Burridge Woods with the river below you on the right.

You will soon see signposts to Marsh Bridge, before joining a lane at Kennel Farm that will take you to the road bridge across the Barle. More excitingly you cross the old packhorse bridge, then trudge uphill, up Looseall Lane, following signs to Court Down. This track passes through woodland, eventually levelling out at a T-junction where you turn right. It's now downhill all the way to Dulverton, with signposts to keep you on track.

(1 Fore St) with a colourful display of all manner of fruit and vegetables, and a farm shop opposite the Bridge Inn that sells fresh produce and snacks. Art lovers old and young, or anyone searching for quality crafts, should take a look at **Number Seven** (7 High St ✆ 01398 324457 ⌂ numbersevendulverton.co.uk ⊙ 10.00–17.00 Tue–Sat, 11.00–16.00 Sun) which, as well as its cards, books and arty items, hosts the outstanding illustrator Jackie Morris and other artists. I particularly liked the 'textile taxidermy' by Helly Powell.

Also not to be missed is **Tantivy** (✆ 01398 323465 ⌂ tantivyexmoor. co.uk ⊙ 06.00–18.00 daily), a super delicatessen and general store with a large selection of local beers and ciders, and a good range of maps and books as well as picnic supplies – so you'll be all set to head for the moor. But not before you've visited **The Guildhall Heritage and Arts Centre** (✆ 01398 323818 ⌂ dulvertonheritagecentre.org.uk ⊙ Easter–end Oct 10.30–16.30 Mon–Fri, 10.30–13.00 Sat, 14.00–16.30 Sun). Admission is free but donations are appreciated. There are fixed and shifting exhibits here with lots of variety and surprises, like Granny Baker's Kitchen where, at the touch of a button, the good lady will chat to you about her life and times. The red deer exhibit tells you everything you need to know about Exmoor's iconic animal. In a separate building is a model railway, beautifully made and correct to the last detail. It's Dulverton as it was before the railway was closed, and the little trains purr their way through tunnels and the familiar landscape before drawing to a halt at the station.

The Heritage Centre is linked to the **National Park Centre** with information about Exmoor and a good range of books and maps.

Also in Dulverton is the headquarters of the **Exmoor Society** (34 High St ✆ 01398 232335 ⌂ exmoorsociety.com ◷ 09.00–16.00 Mon–Fri), which has an Exmoor archive and run guided walks.

Each year Dulverton celebrates a Sunday festival, **Dulverton by Starlight**, in early December; the town is decorated, the shops stay open, there's an evening fireworks display from the church tower, and other events are held to help get people into the Christmas spirit. More information is available on ⌂ dulvertonbystarlight.co.uk.

⑂ FOOD & DRINK

The Bridge Inn 20 Bridge St ✆ 01398 324130 ⌂ thebridgeinndulverton.com. A pub in a wonderful location with exceptionally good food. They specialise in pies, but there is a good choice of other classic dishes. It also has an impressive selection of craft beers and ciders, as well as single malt whiskies.

Copper Kettle 21 Fore St ✆ 01398 323697 ◷ 09.00–17.00 Mon–Sat. A varied and tasty menu, and a Wednesday roast (since they're closed on Sundays). Very popular so can get busy.

Hinam Farm A few miles west of Dulverton in the Barle Valley, TA22 9QQ ⌂ hinamfarmexmoor.co.uk ◷ 11.00–16.30 Wed–Sat, noon–17.30 Sun. 'Definitely the best cream teas and Sunday lunches on Exmoor' says a local friend, and few would disagree with her. Booking essential for Sunday lunch. If you don't want to drive the narrow lanes it's a lovely three-mile riverside walk from Dulverton.

Mortimer's 13 High St ✆ 01398 323850 ◷ 09.30–17.00 Thu–Tue. Good, hearty breakfasts and lunches and an impressive array of specialist teas. And, unlike so many tea rooms, they're open at tea time!

Tongdam Thai 26 High St ✆ 01398 323397 ⌂ tongdamthai.co.uk. My 'man on the spot' reports: 'I rate this very highly. Can appreciate that visitors do not come to Exmoor for Thai food – but it is a real treat for locals.'

Woods 4 Bank Sq ✆ 01398 324007 ⌂ woodsdulverton.co.uk ◷ noon–14.00 & 18.00–

23.00 Mon–Sat, noon–14.00 Sun. Many of the ingredients come from the owner's farm. The restaurant is Exmoor rustic inside: red deer antlers, open fires and sporting prints on the walls. You have the choice of the bar menu served from 18.00 or the pricier full menu later, which specialises in creative ways of using local produce. They also have a very extensive wine list.

37 EXMOOR PONY CENTRE

📞 01398 323093 ✎ exmoorponycentre.org.uk ⊙ Feb–Oct 10.00–16.00 Mon, Wed, Fri & Sun

About four miles west of Dulverton, close to Tarr Steps, is the hamlet of Ashwick and the Exmoor Pony Centre, home of the Moorland Mousie Trust (named after one of the most popular pony books of all time, published in 1929). This charity was set up to give the surplus foals from moorland-bred herds a future by training them to be useful

EXMOOR INTERNATIONAL DARK SKY RESERVE

Exmoor is rightly proud of being Europe's first such reserve. It took a combined effort to achieve this, with the Exmoor National Park, two county councils and Exmoor landowners working together to reduce light pollution.

We can all look up on a moonless night at the thousands of stars visible to the naked eye and say 'Wow!', but, like all things in the natural world, you need an expert to show you what you're seeing and explain its significance, and you need a telescope.

I achieved both on a wonderfully clear (and cold!) night in September when I went to West Withy Farm, which has become the centre for stargazing in southern Exmoor. Seb Jay, Mr Telescope himself, was there with his Dobsonian reflector telescope and his infinite knowledge of infinity. My own knowledge was limited to recognising the Plough, or Big Dipper, and that was about it. The first *eureka* moment was identifying the North Star and then the nearby constellation of Cassiopeia. It helps when

stars form recognisable patterns (such as a saucepan or dipper for the Plough and a W for Cassiopeia). I shall remember those and they're visible to the naked eye. Seb explained that Saturn had just set below the southwestern horizon, which was a shame because its rings definitely have the wow factor, but we were soon transported a brain-numbing distance to two galaxies called Messier 81 and Messier 82, which Seb told me were 11.8 million light years away. In comparison the Andromeda galaxy was a baby at 2½ million light years. Remember that light travels at close to 200,000 miles per second, and do the maths. If distance wasn't enough to cause brain shut-down, the oldest cluster of stars we looked at was the Hercules globular cluster, which is a whopping 12.7 billion years old.

Is there any other word but mind-boggling? Here's the huge sweep of Exmoor sky, and Seb can not only identify but give the vital statistics of everything up there! I asked him

family ponies, so lovers of this distinctive native breed (see box, page 126) get a chance to meet them face to face and perhaps 'adopt' a pony to help with its upkeep. There's an informative display about the Trust in the Green Room.

Experienced riders under the weight of 12 stone (76kg) can book a two- or three-hour trek on Exmoor. See the website for further details.

WALKS IN THE DULVERTON AREA

The National Park Centre has maps and walking guides to inspire you, although if you want to follow the River Barle to Tarr Steps, as suggested by the signpost, you would do better to start from Withypool, from where a footpath hugs the bank the whole way. From Dulverton it is

how he got into it. 'I grew up in North Wales which was pretty dark, so when Mum heard that there was to be a total eclipse of the moon she let me stay up late to see it. We looked at it through binoculars – and I was hooked! I bought a cheap telescope and a wobbly tripod and saw Saturn. Wow! That led to a better telescope, while I was still a teenager, and my doing careful drawings of what I saw so I could learn about it.' Seb studied geology at university, and in 2009 decided to set up his own star-related

business, which eventually led him to become one of the few companies in England to hire out telescopes – and knowledge.

I know I'll only retain a tiny proportion of what I was told that night, but I will look at the night sky with a new appreciation and a little bit more understanding. It's a start.

Seb Jay now sells Dark Sky vouchers, which have proved very popular. His *Exmoor Dark Skies: Our Window into a Universe of Fragile Starlight* is the definitive book for stargazing on Exmoor.

Where to go stargazing

Dark Sky Festival Held over two weeks in October ⊘ exmoor-nationalpark.gov.uk. Over 40 events taking place at venues all over Exmoor, from stargazing talks to night-time adventures.

Exmoor National Park Centres Dulverton, Dunster and Lynmouth. Enquire about hiring a telescope, and perhaps Seb Jay himself, for a special event.

West Withy Farm (⊘ exmoor-cottages.com). This is the complete package with accommodation, Seb Jay and a big white telescope.

Wimbleball Lake The campsite here, with its transparent roofed bell tents, is ideal for stargazing.

KEITH TRUEMAN

"Here's the huge sweep of Exmoor sky; Seb can not only identify but give the vital statistics of everything up there!"

a longer and more complicated route. The circular walk in the box on page 118 gives you a taste of the local scenery in just over three miles.

38 WIMBLEBALL LAKE & HADDON HILL

Wimbleball Lake Activities Centre, TA22 9NU ✆ 01398 371257 ⏺ southwestlakes.co.uk

East of Dulverton is the huge expanse of water that is **Wimbleball Lake**. This reservoir has been developed into a country park with all sorts

Haddon Hill, Wimbleball Lake & River Haddeo

❊ OS Explorer map OL9; start: car park off the B3190 ♥ SS969285; 6 miles; or from Bury village for a slightly shorter walk; moderate to strenuous with a long descent & often muddy ascent

This heath and river walk has splendid views over the lake but only meets it briefly by the dam. Its main focus is a gentle woodland stroll adjacent to the river, with a final muddy uphill slog back to the car, which is why the alternative starting place at Bury has its merits: it gets the uphill over with at the beginning and is slightly shorter.

From the car park, the easiest way to descend to the lake is by using the service lane to the dam. Walk back towards the road and you'll see it signposted 'Wimbleball Dam', on your left; it's an easy descent. The dam is an impressive sight and worth walking across for the lake views or a longer diversion if you want a snack at the café (page 127). Otherwise, follow the signpost to Hartford along the tarred track, Lady Harriet's Drive, to a grassy footpath on the left between wooden railings, marked with blue paint, which leads to the footbridge over the river.

An alternative, and prettier, route from the car park takes in the highest point, **Hadborough**, before dropping down the steep heathery hillside to the lake. One of several paths to Hadborough starts from the lower loop of the car park; this will take you straight up to the trig point but you can use any of the paths and just aim for the highest point. After admiring the view, find the best way down the hillside to the lake. As long as you keep going downhill you will get there in the end and can pick up Lady Harriet's Drive.

Hartford, across the footbridge, is a collection of houses dominated by Hartford Mill and a fish hatchery. The track to Bury, two miles away, is signposted and then it's an easy, level walk along the stony bridle path beside the River Haddeo, with bluebells and primroses in the spring and plenty of birdlife. I was thrilled to see a goldcrest and a dipper.

Bury is a charming small village (no pub, alas!) with a ford and picturesque medieval bridge. Cross this and continue uphill to the bridle path on the left, shortly before a phone box. This is Haddon Lane, an old Devon green road, which after rain is more of a stream than a track. It's

of water and land activities in pleasant surroundings. Above the lake, networked with paths and beloved of dog walkers, is the gorse- and heather-covered Haddon Hill with splendid views over the reservoir and beyond, and a rewarding walk down to Wimbleball and through woodland along the River Haddeo (see box, below).

Wimbleball Lake is all about watersports. It's the leading centre for freshwater activities in the region, and you can learn just about any

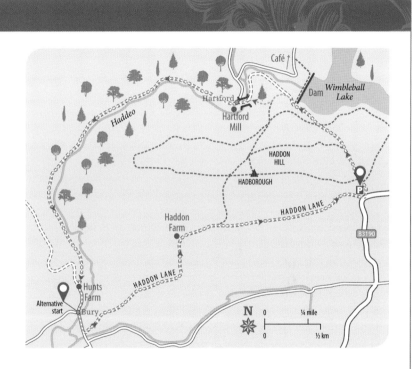

a tough muddy uphill slog between high banks for a bit under a mile before it levels off at Haddon Farm and its access track. About 100 yards after the farm look for a footpath on the left signposted Hartford. This will take you on to **Haddon Hill**, where you leave the footpath to head up to Hadborough along any small path to your right and continue back to the car park.

If you left your car at Bury you will be relieved to know that you have finished with the mud and the climb. After the optional climb to Hadborough, return to the footpath and follow it to Hartford and the footbridge, and thence along the river to Bury.

EXMOOR PONIES

Victoria Eveleigh

The most obvious thing about Exmoor ponies is that they all look remarkably similar – short and hairy, with brown bodies that are dark on top and lighter underneath, dark legs and hooves and a characteristic 'mealy muzzle' (an oatmeal colour over their muzzles and round their eyes). White markings are not permitted on registered Exmoor ponies.

The distinctive colour of the Exmoor pony has led people to believe that it is a direct descendant of prehistoric wild horses, but neither recent genetic research nor studies of documentary evidence support this view. However, it is still a valuable and rare native pony breed.

During the early 20th century it became fashionable to 'improve' native ponies with Arab and Thoroughbred bloodlines, so in 1921 several local breeders got together and formed the Exmoor Pony Society with the purpose of keeping the breed true to type.

The ponies nearly died out during World War II; most of them were killed for food, leaving only about 46 mares and four stallions, but the local farmers soon re-established their herds with the help of a remarkable lady called Mary Etherington.

Today there are about 300 free-living Exmoor ponies on the moor and about 1,300 worldwide, but only a fraction of these are used for breeding. There are 20 moorland herds on Exmoor, including two owned by the Exmoor National Park Authority. All the Exmoor pony herds that graze the different

water-based sport here (kayaking, canoeing, stand-up paddleboarding, sailing and windsurfing), or you can hire a rowing boat or dinghy. There's also a fish farm so you can try angling for trout. If you don't want to go in or near the water there's archery, as well as climbing and high ropes, which have been described as aerial trekking.

A path runs right round the lake making an eight-mile walk but it is probably more rewarding to combine a visit to the shore with Haddon Hill and the Haddeo River. Note that dogs must be on leads by the lake and are not allowed in the water (remember, this is a reservoir).

Haddon Hill is typical high moorland – indeed, one of the highest in eastern Exmoor. It is rich in flora and fauna, providing the perfect habitat for a variety of insects, including the rare heath fritillary butterfly, and a range of birds.

Haddon Hill and its high point, Hadborough, has its own car park where the B3190 makes a right-angled turn near the southern end of Wimbleball Lake. From here you have the choice of a gentle uphill walk to the trig point at Hadborough, 1,165 feet above sea level, for the fine

areas of moorland are free-living (not truly wild, like red deer) because they are owned by farmers with grazing rights on the moorland. For most of the year the ponies fend for themselves, but in the autumn they are rounded up and the foals are weaned and inspected. Until recently all foals that passed inspection had to be branded, but microchipping is now allowed as an alternative to branding.

Exmoors are well camouflaged in their natural moorland habitat. However, you will have a good chance of spotting them on Haddon Hill, Winsford Hill, Withypool Common, Porlock Common, Dunkery Hill, Countisbury, Ilkerton Ridge and Brendon Common. Please don't try to feed the ponies as it encourages them to associate cars with food, which means they are more likely to be victims of a traffic accident. Also, ponies can be dangerous if they start fighting over food.

The Heritage Exmoor Pony Festival (⌀ mepbg.co.uk) is held from August to the end of September, with events ranging from photography workshops to guided walks to see the ponies.

If you would like to see ponies at close quarters, and perhaps ride one, visit the Exmoor Pony Centre at Ashwick, near Dulverton (page 120). And for more information about the ponies, or if you are interested in buying one, the Exmoor Pony Society website (⌀ exmoorponysociety.org. uk) is a useful starting point.

view over the lake, returning along a different but parallel path; or a more rugged, scenic six-mile walk (see box, page 124). Exmoor ponies can usually be seen on Haddon Hill doing their job of keeping the heathland under control.

¶¶ FOOD & DRINK

Coffee Couture @ Wimbleball Lake Signposted at the entrance to Wimbleball ☉ Apr– Oct 10.00–16.00 Wed–Sun, daily in school hols. A pop-up café with a tasty menu of snacks and baking.

The George Brompton Regis TA22 9NL ⌀ 01398 371273. A friendly local pub in this small, high village. Whopping helpings of traditional fare.

UPDATES WEBSITE

You can post your comments and recommendations, and read the latest feedback and updates from other readers online at ⌀ bradtupdates.com/exmoor.

EXMOOR ADVENTURES

We are the area's leading provider of adventurous activities for all ages & groups. Activities include kayaking & paddle-boarding tours, mountain biking trips, coasteering, rock climbing, archery, axe throwing & tree climbing.

Old Bus Garage
Porlock Weir
TA24 8PE

07976 208279
info@exmooradventures.co.uk
www.exmooradventures.co.uk

EXMOOR WILDLIFE SAFARIS

Safaris operate all year round from Exford, Dulverton & Dunster.

Tel: 07977 571494   Email: exmoorwildlifesafaris@gmail.com
Web: www.exmoorwildlifesafaris.com

STEAM TRAINS
at
WOODY BAY STATION

Two-mile Round Trip **PAY ONCE Ride All Day** **Under 5s TRAVEL FREE**

Reviving North Devon's Lost Railway Heritage

© Robin Coombes

ALL STEAM SERVICE - HERITAGE CARRIAGES
WWW.LYNTON-RAIL.CO.UK

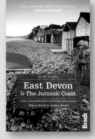

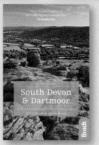

EXFORD BRIDGE TEA ROOMS

Come and visit us for delicious homemade cream teas, cakes, barista coffee, full breakfasts, lunches and bountiful afternoon teas. All our food is freshly prepared using carefully sourced local products, making our menu a taste of Exmoor!

Exford Bridge Tea Rooms
Chapel Street, Exford
Somerset, TA24 7PY

01643 831304
exfordbridgetearooms@gmail.com

WILD ABOUT EXMOOR

Experience Exmoor to the max! Let us be your guides to this very special little piece of England that we are proud to call home. Bespoke opportunities to suit all budgets – just get in touch!

Spindrift Barn, Southcott
Exford, Somerset
TA24 7LY

Part of
**The English
National Park
Experience
Collection**

01643 831759
info@wildaboutexmoor.com
www.wildaboutexmoor.com

QUINCE HONEY FARM

Nestled in amongst acres of wildflower fields, Quince Honey Farm is situated in South Molton 'The Gateway to Exmoor'.

A family run working honey farm and tourist attraction offering a full day out for the whole family. Relax in the nectar gardens while listening to the bees buzz or go wild in the play hive.

The farm restaurant offers delicious homemade dishes made with locally sourced ingredients. The farm shop is where you will find products from our own hives which are located all over North Devon & Exmoor.

During your visit you may wish to take a tractor tour to visit our apiaries and see our beekeeping firsthand before attending one of the daily honey tasting sessions. Visit Quince Honey Farm and taste the countryside!

Visit us:
South Molton,
Devon, EX36 3RF

quincehoneyfarm.co.uk

Call:
01769 572401

Email:
hello@
quincehoneyfarm.co.uk

WELLHAYES VINEYARD

Sample quality sparkling wine produced by a family-run vineyard from grapes grown on site.

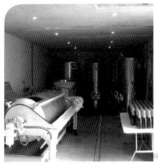

Wellhayes Vineyard
Clayhanger, Devon
EX16 7NY

01398 361612
info@welllhayesvineyard.co.uk
www.wellhayesvineyard.co.uk

THE OLD RECTORY HOTEL

A quiet boutique retreat with great food on the Exmoor Coast.

An award-winning, stylish, country-house hotel set in acres of private gardens close to the stunning and unspoilt Exmoor coast – a true haven in which to unwind and escape from the stresses of everyday life. We have no crowds or traffic to disturb the peace; just birdsong and jaw-dropping scenery.
We delight in creating exciting cuisine utilising the very best local produce which is delicious, fresh, of the highest quality, and very low in food miles.
If you're looking for somewhere to relax and soothe the mind, you really couldn't choose a better place.

The Old Rectory   THE OLD RECTORY HOTEL   01598 763368
Martinhoe, Parracombe reception@oldrectoryhotel.co.uk
Devon, EX31 4QT   www.oldrectoryhotel.co.uk

HIGHCLIFFE HOUSE

A luxury 5-star bed & breakfast on the Exmoor coast
with stunning views over Lynton and beyond.

6 beautifully decorated and luxuriously appointed rooms.
Award-winning breakfast and hospitality.

Tel: 01598 752235 | www.highcliffehouse.co.uk

135

EXMOOR COUNTRY HOUSE

Located within the glorious Exmoor National Park, the house is set in its own grounds nestled between the coast and the rolling landscape of the park. We have a licenced lounge and offer guests the option of evening dinner. Ample free car parking and secure storage for bikes.

Minehead Road,	01643 863599
Porlock	info@exmoor-house.co.uk
Somerset, TA24 8EY	www.exmoor-house.co.uk

HOME PLACE SPA

Adult-only short breaks in your own cottage with breakfast and dinner available.

Home Place Farmhouse Spa	01598 763283
Challacombe, North Devon	info@farmhousespa.co.uk
EX31 4TS	www.farmhousespa.co.uk

EXMOOR CHARACTER COTTAGES

Luxury self-catering holiday cottages in the heart of Exmoor

Stay in luxury period cottages. The Oval in Dunster, Pilgrim Corner, Stone Barn and The Old Sweet Shop in Minehead are perfectly located to explore Exmoor. Each luxury self-catering cottage has its own unique character, complete with original features. The old sits side-by-side with the new, including high-speed Wi-Fi, fully equipped kitchens and high-quality furnishings. Sleeping from five to eight, our three cottages in Minehead have hot tubs. We cater for all ages. Dogs welcome.

For more information, please contact info@exmoorcharactercottages.co.uk
www.exmoorcharactercottages.co.uk
Tel: 07817 698366 or 07943 542657

GORSE COTTAGE

In the heart of Exmoor National Park, Gorse Cottage is a well-appointed self-catering cottage in the village of Withypool. Sleeps up to 6. Dogs welcome. This is a great base for exploring Exmoor with walks from the door. Come and see for yourself!

Gorse Cottage
Withypool

Gorse Cottage

07976 373577
gorsecottagewithypool@btinternet.com
www.withypoolgorsecottage.co.uk

HILLWAY FARM

Hillway Lodge is located in the heart of Exmoor National Park close to the village of Withypool which has a good shop & pub. With lovely views over moorland to the River Barle, our light & warm cottage sleeps 6. Wildlife abounds, the Two Moors Way passes the gate & we have a small herd of Exmoor ponies.

Hillway Farm
Kitridge Lane, Withypool
Nr Minehead, Somerset, TA24 7RY
Email: info@hillwayfarm.com   Web: www.hillwayfarm.com

WOODCOMBE LODGES & COTTAGES

Set in large gardens with fabulous views, this family-run accommodation consists of 6 4-star lodges & 2 cottages sleeping 2 to 10. Games room, putting green, laundry, Wi-Fi. Dogs permitted. Situated near Minehead & Exmoor, 20mins' walk (5mins' drive) to the centre & the beach beyond.

Bratton Lane,
Minehead, Somerset
TA24 8SQ

01643 702789
woodcombelodges@outlook.com
www.woodcombelodges.co.uk

HINDON ORGANIC FARM

Lovely 18th-century farmhouse on a 500-acre, award-winning Exmoor organic farm. Dog-friendly B&B accommodation with local organic produce, walks from the door, breathtaking views and outdoor hot tub.
Real Farm - Real Food - Relax

Hindon Organic Farm
Nr Selworthy, Exmoor National Park,
Minehead, Somerset, TA24 8SH

Tel: 01643 705244
Email: info@hindonfarm.co.uk
Website: www.hindonfarm.co.uk

Little *Quarme* Cottages

Six, cosy, comfortable, self-catering holiday cottages on Exmoor sleeping 2-6 people.

Only 10 minutes' walk across the fields from Wheddon Cross village with pub, shop & garage.

Car-free access to the footpaths & bridleways of Exmoor. You can walk to Dunkery Beacon from your cottage along footpaths & lanes.

Easy driving distance to local attractions including the stunning Exmoor cliff-top coastline, Tarr Steps, medieval Dunster village & castle, Porlock, the Valley of the Rocks, Lynton & Lynmouth.

Great for groups - our barn & games room is perfect for celebration meals & parties.

Dog & horse friendly.

Games for all the family: table tennis, small pool table, croquet, football goal, boules. Large BBQ.

Licensed wedding venue for your exclusive use.

Wheddon Cross, Exmoor National Park, TA24 7EA
01643 841249   www.littlequarme-cottages.co.uk

  Little Quarme Cottages and Weddings

141

STOCKHAM FARM EXMOOR

Luxury farmhouse, self-catering accommodation in the heart of the Exmoor National Park. Two unique, comfortable properties with sensational views close to Dulverton. Sleeping 6 and 4; woodburners; Wi-Fi; dogs and horses welcome; stabling.

Stockham Farm
Dulverton
TA22 9JH

www.stockhamfarmexmoor.co.uk
07785 901017
stockhamfarm@gmail.com

LOCANDA ON THE WEIR

An elegant coastal retreat serving Italian-influenced cuisine with an Exmoor twist. 5 new superior bedrooms with sea views.

Porlock Weir, Somerset
TA24 8PB
01643 863300
www.locandaontheweir.co.uk

INDEX

Entries in **bold** refer to major entries, those in *italic* indicate maps and those in ***bold italic*** indicate photographs.

INDEX OF ADVERTISERS